The **AIDS** Update

Titles in the DISEASE UPDATE series:

The AIDS Update
ISBN-13: 978-0-7660-2746-6
ISBN-10:   0-7660-2746-5

The Asthma Update
ISBN-13: 978-0-7660-2482-3
ISBN-10:   0-7660-2482-2

The Breast Cancer Update
ISBN-13: 978-0-7660-2747-3
ISBN-10:   0-7660-2747-3

The Diabetes Update
ISBN-13: 978-0-7660-2483-0
ISBN-10:   0-7660-2483-0

The Flu and Pneumonia Update
ISBN-13: 978-0-7660-2480-9
ISBN-10:   0-7660-2480-6

The Food Poisoning Update
ISBN-13: 978-0-7660-2748-0
ISBN-10:   0-7660-2748-1

The Sickle Cell Anemia Update
ISBN-13: 978-0-7660-2479-3
ISBN-10:   0-7660-2479-2

The STDs Update
ISBN-13: 978-0-7660-2484-7
ISBN-10:   0-7660-2484-9

The Tuberculosis Update
ISBN-13: 978-0-7660-2481-6
ISBN-10:   0-7660-2481-4

DISEASE
UPDATE

The **AIDS** Update

Alvin and Virginia Silverstein and Laura Silverstein Nunn

Enslow Publishers, Inc.
40 Industrial Road
Box 398
Berkeley Heights, NJ 07922
USA

http://www.enslow.com

Library of Congress Cataloging-in-Publication Data

Silverstein, Alvin.
   The AIDS update / Alvin and Virginia Silverstein and Laura Silverstein Nunn.
      p. cm. — (Disease update)
   Summary: "Discusses the causes, diagnoses, treatment methods,
   and future of AIDS"— Provided by publisher.
   Includes bibliographical references and index.
   ISBN-13: 978-0-7660-2746-6
   ISBN-10: 0-7660-2746-5
      1. AIDS (Disease)—Juvenile literature. I. Silverstein, Virginia B. II. Nunn,
   Laura Silverstein. III. Title.
   RC606.65.S55 2008
   616.97'92—dc22

                                                    2006100475

Printed in the United States of America
10 9 8 7 6 5 4 3 2

To Our Readers: We have done our best to make sure all Internet Addresses in this book were active and appropriate when we went to press. However, the author and the publisher have no control over and assume no liability for the material available on those Internet sites or on other Web sites they may link to. Any comments or suggestions can be sent by e-mail to comments@enslow.com or to the address on the back cover.

Photo Credits: AIDSmeds.com, p. 92; Associated Press, pp. 16, 44, 55, 56, 60, 65, 78, 98, 104, 105; © Chet Gordon/The Image Works, p. 35; © Corel Corporation, p. 68; Gary D. Gaugler/Photo Researchers, Inc., p. 89; James Cavallini/Photo Researchers, Inc., p. 11; Dr. James Oleske, p. 84; Jimmy Zhou/The Emory Wheel, p. 74; Johnny Guaylupo, p. 28; MTV/Courtesy Everett Collection, p. 32; PRNewsFoto/POZ Magazine, p. 8; © Rachel Epstein/The Image Works, p. 51; © Richard Lord/The Image Works, p. 43; Russell Kightley/Photo Researchers, Inc., pp. 5, 24, 40, 103; San Francisco Chronicle, pp. 21, 86; The Soul City Institute for Health and Development Communication, p. 96; © SSPL/The Image Works, p. 48; Time Life Pictures/Getty Images, p. 22; © WHO 2006, All rights reserved., p. 15.

Cover Photo: Russell Kightley/Photo Researchers, Inc.

The cover image shows artwork of HIV, the AIDS virus.

Contents

AIDS

What is it?

AIDS is short for *Acquired Immune Deficiency Syndrome*. It is an illness caused by a virus called HIV that attacks the body's defenses, destroying its ability to fight infections.

Who gets it?

Both genders, all ages, and any ethnic group. Worldwide, the most cases occur in Africa. In the United States and other industrialized countries, it is still most common among gay males and injection drug users. Women and teens are the fastest growing risk groups.

How do you get it?

The virus is transmitted in body fluids. This can occur during unprotected sex. Contaminated needles used for injecting drugs, tattooing, or body piercing can also spread HIV. The virus may be passed from an infected mother to her baby at birth or through breast-feeding. In nonindustrialized countries, blood transfusions may spread the disease. This is rare in industrialized countries.

What are the symptoms?

Fever and flulike symptoms may occur within a few weeks of the initial HIV infection. Later symptoms may include fatigue, swollen lymph nodes, fever, night sweats, frequent yeast infections, skin rashes, diarrhea, memory loss, severe weight loss, Kaposi's sarcoma, and symptoms of infections such as pneumonia (coughing, breathing difficulties, fever).

How is it treated?

A combination of drugs can be used to bring the HIV infection under control. Specific drugs may also be used to treat pneumonia and other infections. A nutritious diet, exercise, and other measures to strengthen the immune system are helpful.

How can it be prevented?

By avoiding high-risk behavior (which includes having unprotected sex, having multiple sex partners, and sharing needles for using injected drugs). Prompt treatment with anti-HIV drugs such as AZT after accidental exposure can help prevent infection. AZT treatment of HIV-infected women during pregnancy can help prevent the spread of the virus to their babies.

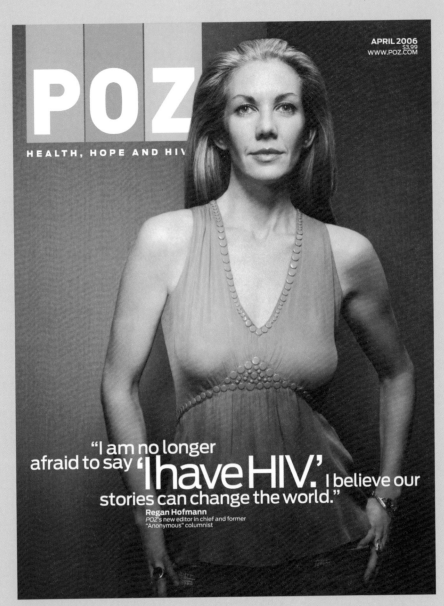

POZ

HEALTH, HOPE AND HIV

"I am no longer afraid to say 'I have HIV.' I believe our stories can change the world."

Regan Hofmann
POZ's new editor in chief and former "Anonymous" columnist

Regan Hofmann announces in a *POZ* magazine cover story that she is HIV-positive. Her announcement helped publicize that heterosexual, middle-class women are at risk for contracting the virus.

1

The Changing Face of AIDS

"I HAVE HIV," Regan Hofmann revealed in the April 2006 issue of *POZ*, a monthly magazine for people living with HIV and AIDS. Normally this announcement would not be surprising, since *POZ* typically contains articles about people with HIV. But Regan Hofmann was not the "typical" face of AIDS—she was a pretty, healthy-looking woman. This image is not what most people picture when they think of someone with HIV, the virus that causes AIDS.

Regan was first diagnosed with HIV in 1996, when she was twenty-eight years old. The year before, her marriage had ended after only eleven months. Then she started dating someone new. Regan admits that she and her boyfriend had unprotected sex twice. Then one day,

Regan became worried when she noticed that she had a very swollen lymph node (an organ that contains disease-fighting cells), so she went to see her doctor. He suggested that the swelling might be due to cat scratch disease, mono, HIV infection, or something else. He took a sample of her blood and sent it to the lab. Regan was not too worried. She was in a one-on-one relationship, and she felt she had not engaged in any risky behavior. When the test results came back, Regan was shocked to find out that she was HIV positive.

Regan did not understand how this could happen. "I had always been very careful," she said. "I had volunteered for Planned Parenthood when I was in high school, I requested that people get tested before I slept with them on occasion. . . . I honestly didn't think I was really at risk."[1] Regan's boyfriend was just as shocked as she was. He then scheduled an HIV test for himself. As it turned out, he was HIV positive as well. Regan's boyfriend told her that he did not know he had the virus. Even though she believed him, they soon broke up. (He died of AIDS complications in 2004.)

Regan started taking HIV medication right away. Her doctor recommended that she join a support group, which was made up entirely of gay men with

HIV. There she was able to talk about her diagnosis freely and felt comfortable knowing that they would keep her secret. She soon subscribed to *POZ*, which helped her a great deal in coping with her condition. Regan did well on the medication. She was relatively healthy. Not many people knew about her condition— only her parents, her sister, and a few friends. When some people wondered about her dramatic weight loss (due to appetite-killing HIV medications), she joked about her diet of stress and caffeine.

Is It HIV or AIDS?

HIV is the name of the virus that causes AIDS. A person can be "HIV positive" (be infected with the virus) but not yet have the actual disease, AIDS. AIDS is the advanced stage of the disease—the stage in which symptoms have appeared. It can take a long time— sometimes ten years or more—before

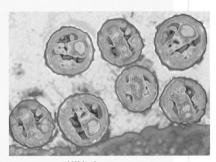
HIV viruses

symptoms of AIDS develop. HIV/AIDS is now commonly used by health professionals to indicate a condition of infection with the virus, whether or not symptoms have appeared.

In 2002 Regan, who had worked as an editor and writer for a number of magazines, began writing an anonymous column for *POZ*. Her articles told about how her HIV status was affecting her life and how people she knew reacted when they learned about it. She was not yet ready to "go public." She knew that many people had negative feelings about people with HIV and AIDS. For a while, she felt ashamed about being HIV positive. Eventually, though, Regan learned to accept her condition and felt better about herself. Four years after she started writing for *POZ*, Regan revealed her name in her column. Her "coming out" feature appeared in an issue of the magazine that had her picture on the cover. By this time, she was the managing editor of *POZ*. [2]

AIDS first appeared in the United States in the early 1980s. The disease was observed mainly in gay white men and drug users. Attitudes toward these people were often harsh and uncaring. Many people believed that AIDS patients were getting what they deserved. In the years that followed, however, the disease spread to other groups in the population. Regan Hofmann is only one example of how the face of AIDS is changing. Most of the people living with HIV/AIDS in the United States

What's in a Name?

These days, when people use the word *gay*, they are talking about a person who is sexually attracted to people of the same sex. Another word for *gay* is *homosexual*. People who are attracted to people of the opposite sex are called heterosexual.

are still gay men and drug users. However, a growing number of HIV-infected people are men, women, and even babies born to HIV-infected women.

What is AIDS exactly? It is a deadly disease that is caused by a virus called HIV (human immunodeficiency virus). The virus attacks the body's defenses until it cannot fight infections effectively. Over time, HIV infection can develop into full-blown AIDS. Ten years ago, a person with HIV was likely to develop AIDS not long after diagnosis, and then die within a few years. Now new drugs are allowing people with HIV to live longer, healthier lives. Some people do not develop AIDS until ten or more years after they became infected.

AIDS is a serious problem all over the world. Two-thirds of all HIV/AIDS patients live in sub-Saharan Africa. Another 20 percent live in Asia and the Pacific.

In 2006, an estimated 39.5 million people worldwide were living with HIV/AIDS. Nearly half of them were women, and more than 2 million were children under the age of fifteen. That same year, there were nearly 3 million deaths worldwide from AIDS-related illnesses.[3] In the United States, over 900,000 Americans were HIV positive; a quarter of them did not even know that they

In 2006, an estimated 39.5 million people worldwide were living with HIV/AIDS. Nearly half of them were women, and more than 2 million were children under the age of fifteen.

were infected.[4] Women accounted for about one-third of the total.

Many people are no longer as afraid of AIDS as they were when it first appeared. Knowing that they can protect themselves from infection—and that they cannot get AIDS through casual contact—has reduced their fears. Health experts believe, however, that some people may now be taking AIDS too lightly. People may decide to have unprotected sex, figuring that they can just take medicine to treat the disease if they get it. But there is

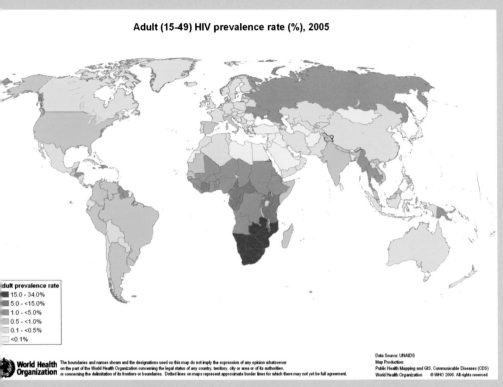

Adult (15-49) HIV prevalence rate (%), 2005

Adult prevalence rate
- 15.0 - 34.0%
- 5.0 - <15.0%
- 1.0 - <5.0%
- 0.5 - <1.0%
- 0.1 - <0.5%
- <0.1%

South Africa has the highest percentage of adults with HIV.

still no cure, and AIDS medications can have some negative side effects. Moreover, the drugs must be taken for a long time—most likely for life. So drugs are not the answer. The key is prevention. Education is the best weapon in preventing AIDS. By learning about the disease and how it is spread, people can lessen their chances of getting infected and infecting someone else.

Dr. Michael Gottlieb shows a model of an HIV-infected cell. Dr. Gottlieb was one of the first to report on AIDS cases.

2

The History of AIDS

IN THE FALL OF 1980, Dr. Michael Gottlieb had just started his new job as an assistant professor at the University of California, Los Angeles. He was looking for ideas for a research project. He asked the doctors he supervised to keep an eye out for any patients with unusual problems involving the immune system, which defends the body against disease. In November, one of the residents told Dr. Gottlieb about a young man with a yeast infection in his throat. It was so severe that the patient could hardly breathe. This kind of infection usually occurs only in people with damaged immune systems. But this patient seemed to be an otherwise healthy young man. Two days later the patient came down with an unusual kind of pneumonia, called Pneumocystis carinii pneumonia (PCP). There was something strange about his blood tests, too. One particular type of white blood cell, called helper T cells, was missing. (White blood cells are the immune system's main weapon in fighting against infections.) Gottlieb wondered what could have knocked out a whole set of immune cells, but he could not find any clues in his medical books.

The patient's medical records showed that he had previously suffered from a number of sexually transmitted diseases (STDs). He also happened to mention that he was gay. At the time, that particular detail did not seem important.

Then, in January 1981, a Los Angeles doctor, Joel Weisman, sent Gottlieb a patient who was having severe immune-system problems. The patient had been running a fever for three months, had persistent diarrhea, fungus infections growing on his fingernails, a yeast infection in his mouth, and severe skin rashes. He had lost thirty pounds. His lymph nodes were swollen, his white blood cell count was very low, and he was having trouble breathing. Tests showed that he, too, had Pneumocystis carinii pneumonia, and he, too, was gay. Gottlieb soon learned of three more gay patients with the same kinds of symptoms. Something unusual seemed to be happening in the local gay community.[1]

Meanwhile, specialists in New York had noticed that several cases of Kaposi's sarcoma had recently appeared in the gay male community there. Kaposi's sarcoma (KS) is a rare kind of cancer. Painless purplish spots that look like a birthmark or bruise appear on the skin. In the United States, KS was normally a very mild, slow-growing cancer that occurred in elderly men. A more serious and rapid-developing form of KS was found in some areas of Africa, however. The New York patients seemed to have this more serious type.

Michael Gottlieb sent a report detailing his cases of PCP to the Centers for Disease Control and Prevention (CDC) in Atlanta. It was published in the June 5, 1981, issue of the CDC's weekly newsletter, *Morbidity and Mortality Weekly Report (MMWR)*.[2]

A New Disease

In the months that followed, more reports about strange cases of illnesses in gay men flooded in. The CDC formed a special task force to study the outbreak. Within a few months, they had more than one hundred cases to study. Some had Kaposi's sarcoma, some had

PCP, and some had both. In addition, some patients suffered from a variety of strange infections. What these varied infections had in common was that they were all "opportunistic." This means they occur only in people whose immune systems are damaged. All of the victims were gay, and most lived in just three places: New York City, San Francisco, and Los Angeles. They typically had many different sexual partners. Most of the men had been treated with medicines for sexually transmitted diseases such as syphilis, gonorrhea, and herpes.

The CDC task force, headed by Dr. James Curran, searched through their disease records. They found no cases of the "gay plague" before 1979—so this was apparently a new disease. But what was causing it? Some researchers thought that the new disease might be caused by a sexually transmitted germ. The CDC team interviewed patients (or relatives, friends, and lovers if the patient had died). They discovered that a group of patients in Los Angeles had some sex partners in common. One patient in New York was found to have been a sex partner of four of the men in Los Angeles, as well as four more of the New York patients. It seemed that some kind of germ had been passed from one patient to another, probably during sex.

"Patient Zero"

Randy Shilts

In his dramatic book about the early years of the AIDS epidemic, *And the Band Played On*, journalist Randy Shilts talked about a French Canadian flight attendant, Gaetan Dugas. Attractive and charming, Dugas had sexual contact with at least forty men among the first 248 AIDS cases reported in the United States. In 1981, Dugas told doctors trying to trace the origin of the disease that during the past ten years he had had at least 2,500 sexual encounters with men he had met in California and New York.[3] Shilts called Dugas "Patient Zero," and the media popularized this label. However, he was not really the "first" AIDS patient, even though he had spread the disease to a number of other men. Dugas himself must have caught it from someone else. Researchers later traced the disease through a number of cases that had occurred earlier, as far back as the 1930s.

Medical researchers began to refer to the new disease as GRID (gay-related immune deficiency), since it affected mainly gay men. Soon newspapers, radio stations, and TV programs all over the country were reporting about this "gay disease." Some religious leaders claimed that the "gay plague" was God's punishment of homosexuals for their lifestyle. Soon, however, the same kinds of opportunistic infections began to appear among other groups of people. Drug addicts who used injected drugs were hit hard by the disease. They included homosexual and heterosexual men, as well as women. Their sex partners—male and female—began to get the disease, too.

Teenager Ryan White became familiar to people all over the world in the 1980s. He had hemophilia, and in 1984 he developed symptoms of AIDS. At school, he had to face prejudice from people who were afraid their children could catch the disease. He became a symbol for the idea that AIDS can strike anyone—even "the kid next door." He worked to educate people about the disease. After his death, in 1990, Congress passed the Ryan White CARE Act to set up health care for people with HIV disease.

Cases also appeared among people who had received blood transfusions. People with hemophilia began to develop the new disease as well. (In

In 1982 the name AIDS (Acquired Immune Deficiency Syndrome) was adopted. Researchers began an active search for the AIDS germ.

hemophilia, the blood does not clot properly, and cuts and scrapes do not stop bleeding. People with hemophilia are treated with "clotting factors," proteins that come from donated blood.) The illness transmitted by blood did not play favorites—it affected people of both genders and all ages, from infants to the elderly. Reports also began to come in from other parts of the United States, and from other countries.

In 1982 the name AIDS (Acquired Immune Deficiency Syndrome) was adopted. Doctors were still not certain this was a single disease, but it seemed increasingly clear that some kind of infection was involved. Researchers began an active search for the AIDS germ.

Discovering the AIDS Virus

From the very first cases of AIDS, doctors had seen that patients had a huge drop in the number of helper

T cells, a particular kind of disease-fighting white blood cell. It seemed likely that the AIDS germ attacked helper T cells. Dr. Robert Gallo, a researcher at the National Cancer Institute in Maryland, was already studying viruses that attack helper T cells. In 1980 he had discovered a virus that causes these white blood cells to multiply uncontrollably, producing a type of leukemia. Gallo thought there might be a similar virus that also attacks helper T cells but destroys them instead of making them multiply. Looking at the blood taken from

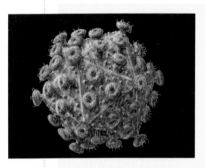

HIV, the AIDS virus

What Are Viruses?

Viruses are the tiniest living organisms on Earth. They are smaller than bacteria. In fact, viruses cannot be seen through an ordinary microscope. Instead, a more powerful microscope, an electron microscope, is needed to see viruses. Viruses need a living organism—a host—to live, grow, and reproduce. They invade body cells and turn them into virus-making factories. When a cell is full of viruses, it bursts open, and hundreds of new viruses spill out. Each new virus finds another cell to invade, and continues the process. Soon there are millions of viruses in the body.

AIDS patients, Gallo's research team found viruses similar to the leukemia virus in several samples.

Meanwhile, a French cancer specialist, Dr. Luc Montagnier, isolated a virus from a patient with swollen lymph nodes; the patient later developed AIDS. Both Gallo and Montagnier described their studies in articles in a May 1983 issue of the journal *Science*. Both research teams began working independently on ways to grow their viruses inside cells in a laboratory dish. They were aiming to develop a blood test for AIDS.

In May 1984, Gallo's research group announced that they had found the virus in forty-eight AIDS patients and had grown large amounts of it in the lab. They had also developed a way to detect antibodies (proteins produced by the immune system to fight the invading germ) that could be used as the basis for an AIDS test. Meanwhile, the French group had developed their own blood test. In 1986 an international committee recommended that the AIDS virus be named HIV (for *human immunodeficiency virus*).

Where Did AIDS Come From?

Most AIDS researchers now believe that HIV first appeared in Africa. Viruses rather similar to HIV have

Researchers believe that today's HIV strains were originally monkey viruses (SIVs).

been found in various kinds of monkeys and chimpanzees from the African rain forests. These viruses, known as SIVs (simian immunodeficiency viruses), do not normally cause illness in monkeys.

Viruses in general—HIV and SIV in particular—have an amazing ability to change. The HIV infecting one AIDS patient may be somewhat different from the virus in another patient. In fact, the AIDS virus in a patient may even change as the infection develops. This ability to change gives the virus a better chance to survive.

Researchers believe that today's HIV strains were originally monkey viruses (SIVs) that were passed to people in Africa, perhaps a century or so ago. We will probably never know exactly how this occurred. Perhaps it happened when monkey blood got into cuts or wounds on hunters who killed monkeys for food.

Biologist Paul Ewald suggests that after SIV passed from monkeys to humans in the African rain forests, the new disease spread slowly. He believes it remained local at first, occurring in just a few villages. After a few decades, though, things changed. Civil wars and industrial development caused people to move from the rural areas into the cities. Often men went to the cities to find work, sending their earnings back to their families in the villages. Lonely and cut off from the tribal traditions, they were more likely to have unsafe sex. Sexually transmitted diseases spread rapidly along the truck routes. The use and reuse of hypodermic needles to give injections of antibiotics and of illegal drugs also spread HIV. Meanwhile, the development of air travel increased the contacts of Africans with people from other continents who came to work or vacation there. The freer sex practices that had become common in places such as the United States were ideal for growing and spreading sexually transmitted germs.

The pattern of an HIV infection is continuing to change. AIDS was very deadly when it first appeared in the United States and other industrialized nations. Gradually, the disease has become more widespread, affecting more groups of people. Meanwhile, education campaigns have stressed the use of protection during sex. Effective tests and treatments were developed. Now the average time between infection by HIV and the development of AIDS symptoms has increased. Even after AIDS symptoms have appeared, people can continue to live productive lives for many years.

AIDS activist Johnny Guaylupo shares his experience of being HIV-positive with other young people and stresses the importance of protection.

3

What Is AIDS?

JOHNNY GUAYLUPO GREW UP in the South Bronx in New York City. As a child, he often felt confused and alone. His dad had left home, and his mom was doing drugs. He was raised by his grandmother. Since his dad wasn't around, Johnny looked up to his uncle, Michael Rivera, who happened to be HIV positive. He knew his uncle was gay and had heard that he became infected because he was an injection drug user.

Johnny was raised Catholic and went to church every Sunday. Sex was not something that was talked about in his household. He was heartbroken when his uncle died of AIDS at age forty. Michael had been the only male role model in Johnny's life. By his early teens,

Johnny realized that he, too, was gay, but he had nobody to talk to about his feelings.

In his sophomore year of high school, Johnny made a new friend, who introduced him to gay life in New York City. Soon he met a thirty-five-year-old man who seemed to be an amazing guy. They started a sexual relationship. At first Johnny and his partner used condoms, but after a while they stopped using them. Johnny did not know much about sex or about the risks of getting STDs. All he knew was that he was in love.

Two years later, at age seventeen, Johnny was still sexually active with the same man. One morning, Johnny woke up with severe stomach pains that lasted all day. He went to the hospital and they ran a few tests, including an HIV blood test. A few days later, he was told that he was HIV positive.

Johnny was too ashamed to tell his grandmother. He needed somebody to talk to, so he went to the school counselor. But the counselor's advice was not very helpful. When Johnny revealed that he was gay, the counselor told him that he was "too young to think about sex."[1]

Johnny's life quickly went downhill. He became depressed and even tried to kill himself. He ended up in the hospital. Johnny was afraid to tell his partner that he was HIV positive. But then at the hospital, he got a phone call from his partner, who admitted to him that he was also HIV positive.

At age nineteen, Johnny felt more alone than ever. He started treatment for his HIV infection but had a very bad reaction to the medicines. At the time, he was in college. He was trying to better his life, but drugs and sex kept getting in the way. After two years, he dropped out of college. He continued to use drugs and ended up in the hospital for depression. He was feeling weak and had night sweats. He had a white blood cell count of only 120 helper T cells. (A normal helper T cell count is at least 1,000.) And his viral load—the amount of HIV in his body—was more than 900,000. He had full-blown AIDS.

Johnny realized it was time to change his life. The first thing he had to do was to get educated about AIDS. He hoped to use this knowledge to help other kids. Johnny joined the Campaign to End AIDS. This program showed him what AIDS was about, and the importance of fighting for people living with the disease.

"I am the face of HIV: I am a twenty-four-year-old gay Hispanic HIV-positive man," Johnny announced at

Famous People with HIV/AIDS

Name	Occupation
Arthur Ashe	Tennis player
Isaac Asimov	Science fiction writer
Esteban De Jesús	World champion boxer
Dan Hartman	Singer and songwriter
Rock Hudson	American actor (first big celebrity to go public about having AIDS)
Michael Jeter	Actor
Magic Johnson	NBA basketball player
Liberace	Pianist
Greg Louganis	U.S. Olympic diver
Freddie Mercury	British lead singer of the rock band Queen
Dack Rambo	Actor
Robert Reed	Actor (Mr. Brady on *The Brady Bunch*)
Pedro Zamora	AIDS educator and character on *The Real World: San Francisco* (MTV reality show)

an AIDS conference in 2005.[2] He regularly attends AIDS conferences and rallies. He tells young people about his experiences and the importance of protecting themselves. In February 2006, he was given the second annual Tasha Durant Award for Positive Leadership. Health-wise, Johnny is doing well and feels positive about his future.[3]

AIDS: The Basics

AIDS is caused by a virus called HIV (*h*uman *i*mmunodeficiency *v*irus). HIV attacks the body by damaging or killing cells of the immune system. The immune system is our body's defense system. It includes several kinds of white blood cells, which protect us against invading germs. When the immune system is damaged by HIV, the body's defenses can no longer fight effectively against infections and cancer. The infections that affect people with AIDS are known as opportunistic infections. They are caused by viruses or bacteria that normally do not cause trouble in healthy people. But they can be very dangerous in AIDS patients because

> AIDS is caused by a virus called HIV.
> HIV attacks the body by damaging or killing cells of the immune system.

their immune defenses are not working effectively. Opportunistic infections that are often seen in people with AIDS include Pneumocystis carinii pneumonia (PCP), tuberculosis, and certain kinds of cancer, including Kaposi's sarcoma.

How Is AIDS Spread?

HIV may be found in all the body fluids of an infected person, especially in the blood and semen or secretions from the vagina. The virus is spread when these fluids are transferred from one person to another. It is usually spread by having unprotected sex with an infected person, mainly through vaginal or anal sex. Like other germs that cause STDs, HIV is passed from the sex organs of one partner to the sex organs or rectum of the other. In some rare cases, the virus has been transferred during oral sex. HIV can infect cells in the lining of the rectum or vagina, or it can pass directly into the bloodstream through a cut or sore.

Many studies have shown that HIV *cannot* be transmitted through casual contact, such as by touching a doorknob or a toilet seat or talking to an infected person. Coughing and sneezing cannot transmit HIV, either. The virus cannot live outside a body for more than a few minutes. Even kissing has not been shown to spread AIDS.

People with another STD, such as syphilis, gonorrhea, genital herpes, or chlamydia, have a greater risk of catching HIV from an infected person. A sore or rash in the genital area provides an easy way for the virus to enter the body.

The AIDS virus can also be passed from an infected mother to her baby during pregnancy or birth. Later, if she breast-feeds, her breast milk may carry HIV into the baby's body.

rse practitioners examine a two-month-old baby who was born to an HIV-infected mother.

The virus can spread through contact with blood as well. Injection drug users may accidentally transfer blood if they share needles to shoot up. Some of the blood from one person remains in the needle and may be injected into the next person who uses it. The virus can then be spread among drug users, and they may then transmit it to their sex partners.

When AIDS first appeared, blood transfusions were also a way of spreading the infection. Now, however, reliable tests for HIV are available, and blood donors are carefully screened. Blood transfusions no longer pose much risk in the United States and other industrialized nations. In some poorer areas of the world, though, needles for blood transfusions or injections of antibiotics are reused without being cleaned properly, and the disease is often spread in this way.

In rare cases, health-care workers have become infected accidentally. This can happen, for example, if they are stuck by a needle containing HIV-infected blood.

Risky Sex

Anybody who is sexually active is at risk for getting AIDS or any other sexually transmitted disease. It can happen to people who have had sex fifty times or to those who are having sex for the first time. It takes only one person infected with the virus to spread the disease. However, the more sex partners a person has, the greater the risk of getting infected. In addition, someone who has an STD has an increased risk of getting an HIV infection as well. But anyone who is in a monogamous relationship—each having sex with just the other person—will *not* become infected with HIV, as long as neither partner carries the virus.

In heterosexual relationships, women have a greater risk of infection than men. For one thing, it is easier for germs to enter a woman's body during sexual intercourse. A man sends his semen, which may contain HIV, directly into the woman's body. There it is warm and moist, the perfect breeding ground for germs. In contrast, most of the woman's body fluids remain on the outside of the man's penis and on the surrounding area, and germs are less likely to get inside.

HIV is more likely to spread during anal sex than vaginal sex. This is because the blood vessels in the rectum are close to the surface, making it easier for the virus to enter the bloodstream.

Becoming HIV Positive

When you get a cold or the flu (both of which are caused by viruses), the body's immune system works hard to protect you from the harmful germs. When viruses enter your body, cells damaged by the viruses release chemicals. These chemicals act as alarm signals, calling in several kinds of white blood cells. Some white blood cells gobble up invading viruses, destroying them before they can infect more cells. Others are able to recognize foreign chemicals—those that are not normally found in the body—such as the proteins on the outer coat of a virus. Some white blood cells produce antibodies, proteins that fit onto virus proteins. Antibodies attach to viruses, preventing them from attacking their target cells and making them easier to destroy.

Once a person has antibodies that protect against a particular virus, his or her body will be able to prevent future infections by it—the person will have become immune to that disease. Some of these specific antibodies continue to circulate in the blood for years, ready to leap into action against attacks by the same type of virus. It generally takes about two weeks to make enough antibodies to fight a virus the body has never met before.

Usually the defending white blood cells do a good job keeping you healthy. But in AIDS, the very thing that is supposed to protect you—the immune system—is being attacked directly. When the body's own defense system is the target, it becomes very difficult for it to fight off infections the way it is supposed to.

What happens when a person is infected with HIV? When HIV gets inside the body, white blood cells are called to fight it. Some attack the virus directly. Others, called B cells, make antibodies against it. White blood cells called helper T cells help the B cells to make the right antibodies. Helper T cells also help other white blood cells, called killer T cells. These killers attack cells that have been infected by viruses, which prevents the infection from spreading. But HIV is tricky. It attaches itself to a protein, called CD4, on the surface of some of the white blood cells. This protein allows the virus to slip inside the cell.

HIV can invade several kinds of white blood cells, but it does the most damage to helper T cells. Once inside the white blood cell, HIV turns it into a virus-making factory. The virus forces the helper T cell to make copies of HIV's hereditary instructions (genes). The completed copy of HIV genes will be copied again

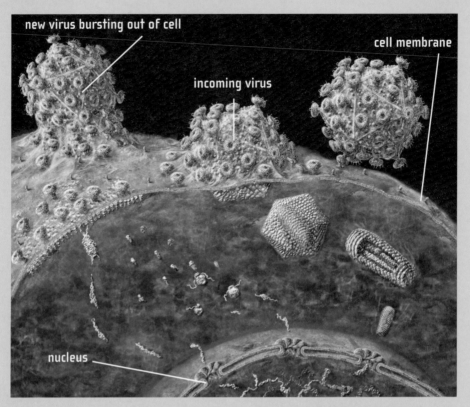

new virus bursting out of cell

cell membrane

incoming virus

nucleus

This illustration shows an incoming virus particle invading a cell. After attaching to the cell membrane, a "package" containing the HIV genes (RNA, yellow) and some proteins enter the cell. An enzyme (green) makes DNA copies (red) of the HIV genes, which enter the cell nucleus. New RN made in the nucleus carries a message to cell structures called ribosomes (orange), which then make new virus proteins. They guide the production of new HIV particles, which burst out of the cell, picking up an outer covering torn from the cell membrane.

every time the T cell divides. For a while, nothing much may seem to be happening, as the virus remains quietly inside the infected white blood cells.

Then, if the body is invaded by new disease germs, the immune system goes into action. As the white blood cells get ready for the fight, HIV gets active too. It tricks the helper T cells into furiously making more copies of virus genes and building new virus particles. Soon each helper T cell is packed with thousands of HIV particles. Then it bursts open, and the new virus particles spill out. They travel through the body fluids to find other healthy T cells and attack them in turn. As the process is repeated, much of the army of white blood cells is wiped out.

What Are the Symptoms?

Many people do not develop any symptoms when they first become infected with HIV. Others may come down with a flulike illness within about three to four weeks. The symptoms include fever, headache, tiredness, and swollen lymph nodes; these usually go away within a week or so. This early stage of HIV infection is often confused with other viral infections, such as a bad cold or flu. The person is very contagious during this time, because the body fluids contain large amounts of virus.

Then, for up to ten years or more, the person may have no apparent symptoms. The person may not even know that he or she is infected. During this time, the person can still pass the virus to others. The virus is very active—multiplying, infecting, and killing cells of the person's immune system.

As the HIV infection gets worse, other symptoms start to develop. More lymph nodes become swollen because the body is battling the multiplying virus. Loss of appetite, fever, rashes, night sweats, and fatigue are other typical symptoms of AIDS. The person may also develop memory loss, confusion, and various other mental problems if the virus has infected the brain. As the immune system weakens, opportunistic infections and certain kinds of cancer may develop. Another common effect is the HIV wasting syndrome, a severe loss of weight and muscle tissue.

Most of the symptoms typically linked with AIDS are caused not by the infection itself but by the other diseases that develop after HIV has dangerously weakened the body's defenses. Coughing and shortness of breath are symptoms of pneumonia. Rashes and sores on the skin or in the mouth may be caused by fungus or herpesvirus infections. Confusion, memory loss, and other mental problems may be due to HIV infection, but they can also be caused by attack on the brain by the parasite *Toxoplasma*. The purplish spots on the skin of some people with AIDS are signs of Kaposi's sarcoma.

HIV/AIDS Symptom Checklist

Early HIV infection:
Flulike symptoms: fever, headache, tiredness, swollen lymph nodes

AIDS:

❑ Loss of appetite, weight loss

❑ Fever, night sweats

❑ Fatigue

❑ Memory loss, mental confusion

❑ Opportunistic infections, such as Pneumocystis carinii pneumonia (PCP), *Mycobacterium avium* complex (MAC), toxoplasmosis, cytomegalovirus (CMV), herpes infections, and CMV retinitis (which can cause blindness)

❑ Certain kinds of cancer, such as Kaposi's sarcoma (KS), lymphomas, and cervical cancer

❑ HIV wasting syndrome (severe loss of weight and muscle tissue)

Earvin "Magic" Johnson began a campaign in 2006 to stop AIDS within the black community. Here he speaks at a news conference on World AIDS Day.

4

Diagnosis
and Treatment

I N NOVEMBER 1991, basketball superstar Earvin "Magic" Johnson of the Los Angeles Lakers shocked the world when he announced that he was going to retire from professional basketball because he was infected with HIV, the virus that causes AIDS. Johnson explained that he found out about his condition by accident when his application for a life insurance policy was rejected because routine medical tests showed that he was HIV positive. Johnson spoke out honestly, stating that he had become infected by having sexual intercourse with too many women without using condoms. Johnson became a symbol that AIDS can strike *anyone.*

When Johnson was first diagnosed, doctors told him

that he had only a year to live. At the time, being HIV positive was basically a death sentence. For a while, Johnson was feeling really upset and discouraged about his future. But he became hopeful after talking with AIDS activist Elizabeth Glaser, who was dying from the disease. (She was the wife of Paul Michael Glaser, who played Dave Starsky in the '70s hit show *Starsky and Hutch*.) Elizabeth had some encouraging words for Johnson: "You are going to be here a long time," she told him, "because we have some great drugs coming down the pipeline. The only thing I want you to do is make sure you go out and talk about HIV and AIDS all the time and help other people."[1] He found that she was right. In the years that followed, new drugs were developed. By 1998, Johnson's immune system was strong, and the amount of HIV in his blood was too small to be detected.

When Johnson first started treatment, there was only one drug available to treat HIV infection: AZT. In 2005, however, there were more than twenty. Johnson used to take fifteen pills three times a day. By late 2006, he was down to three pills twice a day. "The reason I am doing well is because of the drugs," he said in an interview in 2005.[2] He has also learned the importance of staying positive. He stays in shape physically as well. He exercises every day and eats a healthy diet, which includes mostly fish, chicken, and plenty of fruits and vegetables. He has also dedicated his life to educating young people about AIDS and how to prevent it, spreading the word about the importance of "safe sex." He wants people to know the importance of getting tested, as well. With early detection, people infected with HIV can live longer, healthier lives.

More than fifteen years after his diagnosis, Magic Johnson looks healthy, and he says he feels great.[3] Some people even think that he is "cured." But there is no cure for AIDS—yet. Even though the virus may not be detected in blood tests, it is still there, ready to emerge if the conditions are right.

Getting Tested

Many people do not think about getting themselves tested for HIV—unless they know that they have been exposed to the virus. Like Magic Johnson, some people find out that they have been infected when they have routine tests done—to qualify for an insurance policy or a job, for example, or during a yearly physical or gynecological exam.

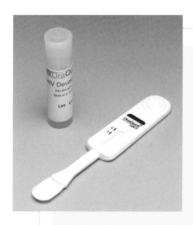

Quick HIV Testing

Medical experts estimate that nearly one million people in the United States are infected with HIV, but about one-quarter of them do not even know they have the virus. Why don't they get tested? Many people are afraid of what the results might be. But by not getting tested, they are putting other people at risk. The fact that blood test results can take up to two weeks to come back has had an impact on who gets tested, as well. "We'd have people get up their nerve to test and then never come back," says health specialist Dr. Kim Thorburn, who works at the Spokane Regional Health District in Washington. HIV tests there are anonymous, so health officials cannot contact these people with the results.[4]

Since the early 2000s, however, HIV testing has gotten a lot faster and easier. The OraQuick HIV test gives results while the patient is still in the health office. The Food and Drug Administration (FDA) approved the test for blood samples in 2002. Later studies showed that it also works with samples of fluid from the mouth, and it was approved as a quick oral test in 2004. A health-care worker uses a cotton swab to wipe along the person's gums, and then places the swab in a special solution. If antibodies to HIV are present, reddish purple lines will appear in a window on the test kit in just twenty minutes. There are no needles involved, and the test is more than 99 percent accurate.[5]

Laboratory tests can detect HIV infection. In the most widely used tests, a sample of blood or saliva is tested for antibodies to HIV, not for the actual virus.

Antibodies to HIV are usually produced within one to three months after infection. However, it may take up to six months for the body to produce enough antibodies to show up in blood or saliva tests. Therefore, even if the test result is HIV negative, the person should get tested again in six months to make sure.

Tests for HIV genes can detect infection earlier than antibody tests can. They are also useful for determining the viral load (how much virus is present in the blood). This information helps doctors decide whether an infected person is likely to develop AIDS. These tests can also help doctors follow how well treatment is working. Tests for HIV genes are not usually used for general screening, however, because they are much more expensive than antibody tests.

When Is It Full-Blown AIDS?

The term *AIDS* is used to describe the advanced stages of HIV infection. The Centers for Disease Control and Prevention (CDC) has developed certain guidelines. First, AIDS is diagnosed in people infected with HIV who have a count of less than 200 helper T cells per cubic millimeter of blood. Remember: Healthy people usually have a helper T cell count of 1,000 or more. In addition, an AIDS diagnosis depends on whether the person has developed any opportunistic infections or certain types of cancer.

The term *AIDS* is used to describe the advanced stages of HIV infection. In addition, an AIDS diagnosis depends on whether the person has developed any opportunistic infections or certain types of cancer.

Drug Treatments

There is no cure for AIDS, but researchers have developed a number of drugs for treating the infection. Doctors have discovered that a combination of several drugs can kill enough viruses to bring the HIV infection under control. These drugs can be used not only for people with active symptoms of AIDS, but also for HIV-infected people who have not yet developed any symptoms. Their viral load may still be small enough that the treatment can kill nearly all the viruses in the body. Then continuing treatments can prevent these

An HIV-positive man pours out his daily "cocktail" of drugs.

people from developing AIDS in the future. Doctors who treat AIDS patients also have a number of drugs for treating opportunistic infections.

The medications that work directly on HIV, rather than on the opportunistic infections, are called antiviral drugs. They belong to three main groups:

• **Nucleoside antivirals** are chemicals that are similar to the building blocks (nucleosides) that HIV uses to build new virus particles. The virus is "fooled" into picking up these drugs instead of their normal building blocks, and then cannot use them for the next steps in the building process. Nucleoside antivirals thus stop HIV from multiplying. AZT, the first drug developed for treating AIDS, belongs to this group.

• **Non-nucleoside reverse transcriptase inhibitors** (NNRTIs) also work to prevent HIV from reproducing, but they are not chemically similar to the virus's normal building blocks. These drugs interfere with the enzyme (reverse transcriptase) that HIV uses to build new virus genes. (An enzyme is a chemical, usually a protein, that makes chemicals react.)

• **Protease inhibitors** are drugs that interfere with an enzyme called protease. This enzyme cuts large proteins into smaller pieces that HIV uses to help build new virus particles.

These three kinds of drugs attack HIV in different ways. Medical researchers have found that they work most effectively when several different types are used together. Remember that HIV is so changeable that a number of different strains (types) of the virus may be present in a person's body at the same time. Picture a patient infected with two strains of HIV. One drug may work better on the first strain. Another drug is more effective against the second strain. Still another drug may knock out viruses that the first two drugs missed. Doctors usually prescribe a combination "cocktail" of drugs that the patient takes every day. This kind of treatment is known as HAART (highly active antiretroviral therapy).

The antiviral treatments may also be combined with drugs to prevent opportunistic infections. Certain antibiotics, for example, can prevent PCP. The most effective combinations of antiviral drugs cannot kill *all* of the HIV in a patient's body, however. Even when lab tests no longer show any traces of HIV, some viruses are still hiding out in the nerves or other tissues. This happens because antiviral drugs generally work only on viruses that are active. If the drug treatments are stopped and then the person gets some other infection, the immune system goes into action. Then some of the hidden viruses "wake up" and start infecting white blood cells—and the disease starts all over again.

AIDS medications are not perfect. They can have some annoying and even life-threatening side effects, from nausea and diarrhea to a dangerous drop in the number of red or white blood cells, and to painful nerve damage. And the drugs must be taken for a long time, probably for life. In addition, AIDS medications do not have the same effect on every person. Everybody is different. A drug cocktail that works very well for one person may not work at all for another.

Many patients find it difficult to stick to their ongoing treatment. It is not easy to remember to take so many pills at different times of the day. Unfortunately, skipping doses can lead to a serious problem called drug resistance. When the prescribed drugs are not all taken when they should be, they are unable to kill enough of the viruses. The "strong" ones survive and multiply, producing a whole population of drug-resistant viruses. Soon the HIV infection returns, and the person becomes sick again. This time, though, the drugs that were used before will no longer work. These drug-resistant strains may be passed on to other people. They will not respond to the drugs, even though the new person had never taken these drugs before.

Once-a-Day AIDS Drug

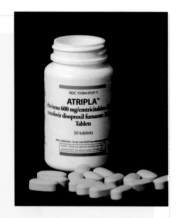

In July 2006, the FDA approved the first once-a-day AIDS drug, called Atripla. It would be used in the United States as well as in a number of nonindustrialized countries. Atripla is a combination of three drugs in one, which means that HIV/AIDS patients will not need to take so many pills. (Before Atripla, the usual treatment typically amounted to twenty or more pills a day.) Medical experts believe that having to take fewer pills will help patients stick to their treatment better, which in turn will lessen the chances of drug resistance.

A ten-month study of 244 HIV-infected people showed that the three-in-one combo drug was effective in 80 percent of the cases. The drug was able to greatly reduce the viral load and increase the number of helper T cells. However, Atripla will not get rid of the need for other medications, such as those that help prevent opportunistic infections. And some people may need to take other HIV drugs along with Atripla to fight the infection effectively.[6]

Bono and Oprah leave a Gap store after a shopping spree that was part of their "Red campaign."

In the United States and other industrialized countries, HIV can be controlled by medications. In nonindustrialized countries, where many people cannot afford these medications, HIV is still killing millions of people every year.

Celebrities are getting involved in raising funds to buy AIDS medications for people in Africa. In March 2006, singer Bono (from the rock group U2) started what he called the Red campaign. The Gap, Armani, Apple, Motorola, and other big companies are giving part of the profits on certain products to help fight AIDS in Africa. In addition, American Express set up a special "red" credit card that gives one percent of every purchase to the Global Fund to Fight AIDS, Tuberculosis, and Malaria. Bono, Oprah Winfrey, and other celebrities have staged "shopping sprees" to help publicize the campaign.[7]

5

Living with HIV/AIDS

HYDEIA BROADBENT HAS been living with HIV literally her entire life. Her mother was an injection drug user and became infected with HIV through contaminated needles. She passed the virus on to Hydeia when she gave birth to her in 1984. Unable to take care of herself, let alone a brand-new baby, Hydeia's birth mother abandoned her at the hospital. Fortunately, Hydeia was adopted when she was six weeks old by a former social worker, Patricia Broadbent, and her husband, Loren.

Hydeia's adoptive parents could not understand why their new baby girl was getting sick so often. "If someone came over with a cold, she got a cold. If she was exposed to someone with strep, she got strep. I just attributed it to the fact that her birth mother was an IV drug user and had no prenatal care," Patricia Broadbent said.[1]

When Hydeia was three years old, her parents got a call from social workers telling them that Hydeia's birth mother had had another child, a boy, who tested positive for HIV at birth. They advised them to get Hydeia tested as well. Hydeia's test results showed that she, too, was HIV positive. The doctors told her parents that she would not live past the age of five.

At five, Hydeia was still alive, but her infection had developed into full-blown AIDS. She was accepted into a pediatric AIDS program, in which she would receive two AIDS medications, AZT and DDI.

Before adopting Hydeia, Patricia knew very little about AIDS. As she learned more and more about the disease, she started giving talks to local groups about the difficulties of raising a child with AIDS. At the same time, Hydeia was soaking up all the information she could, from her mother, doctors, nurses, and other patients. She soon learned that many people had wrong ideas about AIDS, which, in turn, led to fear of those who had the disease. In fact, Hydeia had come face-to-face with these fears when she was only five. Her teacher

Fourteen-year-old AIDS activist Hydeia Broadbent, who was diagnosed with HIV at age three, receives an Essence Award in 1999.

tried to use bleach to kill the virus whenever Hydeia sneezed in class. "My mom always said, 'There's ignorant people and there's stupid people,'" Hydeia said. "'You can always educate ignorant people, but stupid people are just stupid.'"[2]

By age six, Hydeia was on a mission: She wanted to educate people about AIDS. She started talking to groups about what it was like to have AIDS. They needed to know the facts about the disease, she believed, so that they could protect themselves. She didn't want anybody to have to go through what she was going through. By the time she was twelve, she had been on television programs including *Oprah, 20/20, Good Morning America,* and a TV special called *A Conversation with Magic Johnson.* Later she was honored with a Red Cross Spirit Award and a 1999 Essence Award for her efforts toward AIDS awareness. Hydeia has also been interviewed by reporters from a number of publications, including the *New York Times, Essence,* and *Seventeen,* and she was on the cover of *TV Guide* in 2004.

Hydeia has continued to travel and speak out, despite the difficulties of growing up with a disease like AIDS. By the age of nine, she had had pneumonia three times and chickenpox several times. (Her damaged immune system could not protect her against each new infection.) Her mother schooled her at home so that she could take her pills on time and get the ten to twelve hours of sleep she needed each day. Now a college student in her twenties, Hydeia is in relatively good health, although she has some off days. She is still a dedicated AIDS activist, speaking about the disease and her experiences to groups and conferences all over the country. She also has her own national AIDS outreach program that uses hip-hop music to help educate kids with and without HIV.

During her travels, Hydeia has found that many young people these days seem to think that if they get AIDS, they will just take medication and they will be all better. She wants to change that kind of thinking. "[What] I want people to know is that living with AIDS, every day is a struggle," Hydeia said. "You don't have a day off—whether it's dealing with symptoms, or dealing with medications or how you're going to pay for medications. But you can't get stressed about it, because stress makes your symptoms worse. Still you have to try to live positive so you can be healthy. And that's all anyone with AIDS is trying to do."[3] Life is tough enough, she explains, without taking a chance on an illness that is completely preventable.

Still a Stigma?

If someone were to say, "I have diabetes," or "I have asthma," a typical reaction would be sympathy and support for the person with these kinds of diseases. But a person who says "I have AIDS" often gets a completely different kind of reaction—one of fear and blame. Why have people reacted so negatively to those who suffer from such a devastating disease? Don't they deserve sympathy and support too?

Unlike most other diseases, there is a stigma attached to AIDS—that is, people with the disease are made to feel shame. The stigma comes from the fact that AIDS involves some of the things people do not like to talk about openly in society—sex, drug abuse, and homosexuals. When AIDS first appeared, it was commonly believed to be a disease of gay men and drug addicts—and that these people were only getting what they deserved as punishment for their "bad" behavior. In fact, this attitude continued into the next decade. In 1995, Senator Jesse Helms wanted to reduce the amount of federal money for AIDS sufferers because he said it is their "deliberate, disgusting, revolting conduct that is responsible for their disease."[4] What people didn't realize was that this disease would soon become *everybody's* problem.

People with HIV/AIDS have faced discrimination in nearly every aspect of their lives. Some hospital workers have refused to care for them. Insurance companies have refused to pay their medical bills. People with HIV have been evicted from their homes and fired from their jobs. School boards have tried to keep children infected with HIV and even their uninfected family members from coming to school. Some friends and family members have been sympathetic and supportive, but others have abandoned people with AIDS and treated them like outcasts.

People who shun those with HIV and treat them as though they do not belong in society are acting out of fear and ignorance. Attitudes are changing, though *slowly*. By the early twenty-first century, the facts about HIV, AIDS, and sex were being presented and discussed more openly and without embarrassment. People were able to talk freely in public—on television and radio, and in newspapers and magazines—about sex and condom use. In addition, talk shows, movies, and soap

Fighting HIV/AIDS Discrimination

In September 1994, Sidney Abbott went to see her dentist, Dr. Randon Bragdon, to have a simple cavity filled. When she told him that she was HIV positive, Dr. Bragdon refused to treat her in his office. At the time, this was only one in a growing number of cases in which doctors and dentists were refusing to treat HIV-positive people. Sidney was afraid that soon, people infected with HIV would be unable to get medical care, so she took Dr. Bragdon to court.

In front of the U.S. Supreme Court, Sidney Abbott said that Dr. Bragdon violated the Americans with Disabilities Act (ADA). The ADA, signed by President George H. W. Bush in 1990, protects people with disabilities from being discriminated against in the workplace, housing, and health care. Until this time, the ADA included people with full-blown AIDS, but not those who were HIV positive and still symptom-free. Dr. Bragdon argued that since Sidney did not have any symptoms yet, she was not disabled and should not be protected by the ADA. But Sidney explained that she was impaired because her condition limited her ability to have children. The court sided with Sidney Abbott. In 1998, the U.S. Supreme Court stated that people with HIV were covered under the Americans with Disabilities Act, even if they did not show symptoms.[5]

operas were featuring AIDS-related stories. AIDS activists like Hydeia Broadbent and Johnny Guaylupo were working hard to help increase AIDS awareness. Even former Senator Jesse Helms had changed his mind about AIDS. In a book he wrote, *Here's Where I Stand*, published in 2005, Helms talked about his friendships with North Carolina evangelist Franklin Graham and rock singer Bono, who got him interested in the fight against AIDS in Africa. "Until then," he wrote, "it had

> Many HIV-positive people are still afraid to reveal their HIV status because they worry about the reactions of their family and friends. In fact, many of them will not get tested because they are afraid that people will find out.

been my feeling that AIDS was a disease largely spread by reckless and voluntary sexual and drug-abusing behavior, and that it would probably be confined to those in high-risk populations. I was wrong."[6]

Many HIV-positive people are still afraid to reveal their HIV status because they worry about the reactions of their family and friends. In fact, many of them will not get tested because they are afraid that people will find out. However, this creates a dangerous situation. If the infection goes undetected, then those infected will not get the treatment they need to keep the disease from getting worse. In addition, these people may unknowingly spread the virus to others. A 2000 study showed how much of an impact the AIDS stigma has on whether or not people get tested. People who engaged in high-risk behaviors were five to eight times less likely to get tested than people who did not engage in risky behaviors.[7]

Will the AIDS stigma ever go away? It may never be eliminated completely, but as public awareness continues, more and more people will have a better understanding of the disease. If there were no stigma linked with AIDS, those at risk would be more likely to get tested. This would benefit everybody.

Keeping Physically Fit

Living with HIV/AIDS is not all about taking medications. It is also about living a healthy lifestyle. This means getting enough sleep, exercising, and eating the right foods. All these things help to boost the body's immune system. When the immune system is strong,

Exercise keeps the body and mind strong, which in turn helps the body fight infection.

the patient can fight the HIV infection more effectively. A strong body can also help a person handle the AIDS medications better, as well as the side effects.

Exercise is very important. Resting too much can weaken muscles, and the heart has a harder time pumping blood around the body. Physical activity is very important in strengthening the muscles, heart, lungs, and overall circulation. Furthermore, it keeps the whole body strong. People don't need to run two miles a day to be physically fit. Exercise can be as simple as taking long walks—anything that moves the body and temporarily raises the heart rate.

Exercise is good not only for the body but also for the mind. When the body is active, chemicals called endorphins work in the brain to produce "happy" feelings. Exercise can also make people feel good about themselves, giving them a sense of accomplishment and independence. Mental health is especially important for HIV/AIDS patients, since they often go through periods of sadness and frustration.

Getting enough sleep is just as important as getting enough exercise. During the day, people use a lot of energy. Sleep gives the body a chance to rest. While a person is asleep, the body can heal cuts, bruises, and sore muscles. A lack of sleep weakens the body's defenses, which makes it harder to fight disease germs.

HIV/AIDS patients need to watch what they eat as well. A balanced diet that includes a variety of healthy foods will help to strengthen the immune system. It should be high in complex carbohydrates and low in fat, with plenty of protein. Complex carbohydrates help to boost the body's energy level. They may include whole grains (cereals, pastas, rice, flour, and bran), legumes (beans, lentils, and peas), potatoes, and other vegetables. Protein is very important because it is needed to build, maintain, and repair cells. During treatment, the body needs enough protein to repair damaged tissues and to help keep the immune system strong.

Getting Support

HIV/AIDS can be a real test for relationships. Patients are able to cope much better when they have a strong support system, with friends who understand. A supportive family and good friends will help patients through their battle and stick by them no matter what. However, not all relationships can withstand the stresses involved in battling a disease, especially one that still has a stigma attached to it.

Support groups can be very helpful for people with HIV/AIDS. These groups are made up of people who are HIV positive or have full-blown AIDS. Being able to talk about symptoms, fears, and treatment decisions with people who *really* understand can be a

> **Support groups can be very helpful for people with HIV/AIDS.**
>
> **These groups are made up of people who are**
>
> **HIV positive or have full-blown AIDS.**

big help emotionally for someone who has recently been diagnosed or is struggling with side effects or setbacks during treatment. Some support groups meet in person, but telephone and Internet connections are also available.

6

Preventing AIDS

WHEN MARVELYN BROWN was nineteen years old, she thought she had met the man of her dreams. He was an older man, good-looking, smart, and sophisticated. She couldn't believe that such an amazing guy was giving her so much attention. Soon they decided to have sex. However, Marvelyn's partner told her he didn't have any condoms. She didn't want to upset him by saying no because she was afraid that she might lose him. "[I] thought it was a privilege that he wanted to have sex with me," she recalls.[1] So they had sex without any protection.

About two months later, Marvelyn wound up in the hospital after becoming unconscious with a 106-degree fever and pneumonia. The hospital workers ran a battery of tests. Marvelyn thought that the doctors were going to tell her that she was pregnant. Instead, they told her she was HIV positive. Marvelyn realized that she knew very little about her boyfriend's sexual history. Later, she found out that her partner—who looked perfectly healthy—had known that he was HIV positive the whole time.

Like many people, Marvelyn had thought she was safe. "I just thought you could look and tell," she says.[2] She learned the hard way that anyone can get infected, even her charming, seemingly healthy, great-looking guy.

When word got out about Marvelyn's condition in her hometown of Nashville, she was rejected by most of her friends and neighbors. Driven by their strong religious beliefs, these people called Marvelyn hurtful names and judged her harshly for getting infected with this "gay man's disease." Things got so bad that soon nobody wanted to be around her.

Marvelyn decided to turn her depressing situation into something positive. She was going to dedicate her life to educating young people about HIV/AIDS. This is a disease that can be prevented. She had learned the

Marvelyn Brown hopes to break stereotypes about HIV patients.

hard way how important it is for people to protect themselves. Now Marvelyn works at Nashville CARES, educating young people about HIV. She is also a certified HIV testing counselor. She travels across the country to colleges and high schools to talk to both adolescents and adults about her experiences. She also tells them what they can do to avoid getting infected. Marvelyn has become an outspoken AIDS activist. She has been on TV and radio shows, spreading the word about AIDS prevention.[3]

Safer Sex

The only "safe sex" is abstinence. *Abstinence* means having no sexual contact with a partner. Many young people today feel pressured to have sex. They have to deal not only with the pull of their own hormones, but also with the need to feel accepted and to please the one they love. People who think they are ready to have sex need to consider all the possible consequences.

People who choose to have sex with a partner can make it safer by using a rubber condom. A condom is a thin covering that is placed on the penis before having sex. When used properly, condoms are effective in protecting against AIDS and other STDs, as well as

Who's at Risk?

Anyone who is sexually active is at risk for getting AIDS, but certain people have a greater chance of getting infected because of their risky behaviors. These behaviors include:

- Having many different sex partners
- Injection drug use (when needles are shared)
- Sexual activity without using a condom
- History of STDs

pregnancy. They are not foolproof, however, because they can break, tear, or slip off. The chances of a condom breaking, however, are actually very low—2 percent or less.

Having sex is a big responsibility, and it can have unwanted consequences. It is important for people to know what they are getting into. They should find out their partner's HIV status before they have sex. Unfortunately, people may not tell the truth, especially with something like HIV. They may be too embarrassed or they may not want their partner to know. They may not even know they are infected because it can take years for symptoms to develop. The only way to know for sure whether someone is infected with HIV is to get

The Female Condom

Many men do not like to wear condoms, and they often choose not to use them. But women can choose a different type of condom that is made just for them. It is called the vaginal pouch, which was approved by the FDA in 1993. It is actually a female version of the male condom. This female condom gives women the power to protect themselves from AIDS and other sexually transmitted diseases.

tested. It is best not to take chances. If people are going to have sex, they should use a condom every single time. No exceptions—because it takes just one time to become infected.

Clean Needles for Drug Users

Since the AIDS epidemic first started, injection drug users have accounted for about 35 percent of the more than 950,000 AIDS cases that had been diagnosed in the United States by the end of 2005.[4] As discussed, HIV is spread when drug users share needles. During the injection of the drug, the drug user typically draws a little blood into the syringe to make sure the needle is inserted into a vein. If this contaminated syringe is then used by someone else, the blood may be injected into another drug user.

During the 1980s, it was illegal in most states for anyone to have hypodermic needles and syringes without a doctor's prescription. Therefore, without access to sterilized (germ-free) equipment, drug users felt they had no choice but to share their needles and syringes. Addicts often went to "shooting galleries"—apartments or alleyways where they paid a small fee to get privacy and a needle to use. These needles usually contained

The Condom Controversy

Until the 1990s, sex education in schools focused almost entirely on abstinence. There was little or no discussion about other options, such as using condoms, as a way to protect against AIDS and other STDs. As a result, those who did choose to have sex were not educated on how to protect themselves. The lack of proper AIDS education was only helping to spread the disease.

In an effort to fight AIDS, New York City Schools Chancellor Joseph A. Fernandez started a program in 1991. It involved discussions about condoms in the sex education classes of New York public schools. The schools also offered free condoms to any student who wanted them—no questions asked. The program stirred up a lot of controversy, however, because many people felt that the schools were telling kids that it was okay to have sex. Chancellor Fernandez was fired two years after the program started.

In December 1999, the American Medical Association (AMA) stated that teaching abstinence-only sex education in public schools was not helpful in preventing AIDS and other STDs. Studies showed that safer sex programs that included information on both abstinence and condom use did not increase sexual activity among teenagers. In fact, such programs seemed more effective in delaying sexual activity than abstinence-only education.

By 2005, condoms were being offered in most colleges, universities, and public health clinics and in at least 400 high school health offices in the United States.[5] As of 2006, however, the U.S. government was still providing funding just for abstinence-only sex education programs.

traces of blood from a previous user. If the needles contained HIV-infected blood, the virus could be transmitted from one drug user to another. The users could then pass the infection on to sexual partners and even to their children.

In 1988, Yolanda Serrano shocked authorities by creating a program that gave clean needles and syringes to drug addicts in exchange for their contaminated ones. Serrano was the head of a private addiction and AIDS prevention organization in New York City, called Adapt (the Association for Drug Abuse Prevention and Treatment). Although her plan was against the law, she fought for it. The first New York needle-exchange program (NEP) was finally started by the New York City Department of Health. Needle-exchange programs had already been tried successfully in places such as the Netherlands. There, addicts could use automatic dispensing machines that exchange a fresh needle for a used one.

The New York needle-exchange program was anonymous. Addicts could go to neighborhood locations and exchange their contaminated needles for an equal number of sterilized ones. Some needle-exchange sites were located outside a storefront or a parked van.

In other cases, the van roamed the streets or the workers walked around looking for drug addicts. The fixed locations also offered other services such as HIV testing and counseling, tuberculosis testing, and condom distribution.

The needle-exchange program faced a lot of controversy. Critics felt that this program was sending out the wrong message, telling drug addicts that it was okay to use drugs. Studies have shown, however, that NEPs have not increased the amount of drug use in the communities they served. In fact, they have been effective in reducing the risk of spreading HIV.

Needle-exchange programs have since been set up in communities throughout the nation, even though the U.S. government still refuses to fund them. However, it is now legal in most states to buy syringes in pharmacies without a prescription. In 1992, Connecticut was among the first states to pass such a law. In the years that followed, studies showed that needle sharing among drug users decreased by 40 percent in that state.[6] In 2005, state representative Peter Koutoujian supported the bill that made it legal to sell syringes over the counter in Massachusetts. He felt that this move was an important step toward slowing down the spread of

AIDS. "We can no longer afford to put our communities at risk out of a misplaced fear for encouraging drug use," he told critics.[7] By 2006, the number of NEPs had grown to 185 in thirty-six states, as well as in Washington, D.C., and Puerto Rico.[8]

Preventing AIDS in Babies

Every year, an estimated 7,000 HIV-infected American women give birth. Without treatment, about 25 percent of their babies will be born HIV positive.[9] Before the early 1990s, there was little hope for children born to HIV-infected mothers. But in 1994, a study sponsored by the National Institutes of Health (NIH) showed that taking the drug AZT during pregnancy can greatly reduce the risk of mother-to-child transmission of HIV. Researchers found that only 8.3 percent of the babies were likely to become HIV infected if they and their mothers received AZT, compared with 25.5 percent who did not get the drug.[10]

Since 2003, the CDC has recommended that HIV testing be included in the routine prenatal care of all pregnant women, unless they refuse the test. Women who test positive for the virus can then start treatment right away to protect their babies. These days, treatments

Every year, an estimated 7,000 HIV-infected American women give birth. Without treatment, about 25 percent of their babies will be born HIV positive.

include a combination of powerful drugs that are so effective that the risk of mother-to-child transmission of HIV has been reduced to 2 percent or less. In the United States and other industrialized countries, this combination therapy is standard for HIV-infected pregnant women. However, the cost of these drugs is too high for those in the nonindustrialized countries. Such countries account for about 90 percent of the roughly 600,000 HIV-infected babies born worldwide every year.[11]

Another way that HIV-infected women can reduce their risk of passing the virus during birth is by having a caesarean section. This is a surgical procedure in which the baby is born through the mother's abdomen. The procedure helps to protect the baby from coming into contact with the mother's infected blood and other fluids.

HIV Risk at Work

Health-care workers often have to take care of HIV-infected patients. They are in constant contact with the patients' blood or other body fluids. Therefore, they have a risk of becoming HIV-infected through exposure at work. However, the risk has been greatly lowered—to only 0.3 percent—since the CDC required that all health-care workers follow the standard infection control procedures, known as universal precautions.[12] These safety practices include hand washing; wearing wraparound smocks, gloves, and masks; careful handling of needles and other sharp instruments; and strict sterilizing procedures.

Despite the use of universal precautions, an estimated 385,000 health-care workers in the United States are stuck with needles or other sharp instruments each year.[13] It is now standard practice to treat all accidental needlestick injuries with AZT or other anti-HIV drugs. This preventive treatment has greatly reduced the chances of getting infected. Treatment is most effective during the first few hours after exposure.

SPOTLIGHT:
Growing Up with Aids

James Oleske, a New Jersey pediatrician, treated his first baby with AIDS in 1978—before anyone had even heard of AIDS. She was a five-year-old girl with an unusual case of pneumonia, and her immune system was not working properly. She died, but Dr. Oleske kept a sample of her blood. Soon other children came in with unusual health problems and a defective immune system.

When the first cases of AIDS appeared in 1981, no one dreamed of linking these sick children to this new mysterious illness, which was affecting gay men and, later, drug users. But Dr. Oleske found the connection when he discovered that the father of the little girl he had treated a few years earlier was also sick with the same symptoms she had.

In 1983, Oleske published an important article in the Journal of the American Medical Association (JAMA). He was one of the first doctors to show that children could also get this deadly disease. HIV was identified that same year. Dr. Oleske tested the blood sample he had kept since 1978 and found that the little girl had indeed been infected with the virus. By that time, he and his colleagues were already treating close to fifty children with AIDS.

Oleske still has a keepsake to remind him of the early days of the AIDS epidemic. A little boy he had been treating said he thought he was going to die and asked Oleske to take care of his stuffed rabbit. That night, Oleske's phone rang at three A.M. The boy had just died of AIDS. In the morning Oleske found "Old Fred," the stuffed rabbit, in the pocket of his lab coat.

Over the years, he has sadly watched many of his young AIDS patients die. With the effective new treatments, however, Oleske has seen AIDS go from an automatic death sentence to a manageable disease. He still treats about three hundred AIDS patients, many of whom are now teenagers and young adults. One of his original patients recently graduated from medical school and began training as a pediatrician.

After more than twenty-five years as a pediatric AIDS doctor, Oleske is still very active in the field. He is training young doctors from other countries, who will go back to their homelands to treat children with AIDS. He has traveled to a number of countries including Uganda, South Africa, Russia, and India to work with AIDS foundations in those places.[14]

Michael DeLane is enrolled in a gene-altering experiment in which genes producing an antiviral enzyme were inserted into his blood cells.

7

AIDS and the Future

I N APRIL 2006, MICHAEL DELANE had reason to celebrate. It had been one year since he stopped taking all his AIDS medications. Many AIDS patients have tried taking breaks from their medicines, only to find their virus levels eventually going back up. But Michael was one of a small number of people who managed to keep their virus loads low for a year or more. Was Michael just lucky, or was it the result of an experimental study he participated in nearly two years earlier?

After Michael found out he was HIV positive in August 2002, he kept a close eye on AIDS research. He wanted to be among the first to get involved in any experimental studies for promising treatments. In June

2004, Michael got his chance when he participated in an unusual experiment conducted by researchers at University of California, San Francisco (UCSF). The study involved seventy-four HIV-infected men and women. Using the latest technology, half the participants were given a gene that blocks the AIDS virus. The goal was to ultimately make the body's immune system resistant to HIV.

How can this happen? Researchers of the study say the key to controlling HIV is a special enzyme called a ribozyme. This particular ribozyme was created in the laboratory. The ribozyme acts as a kind of chemical "scissors" designed to cut up one of HIV's genes, stopping it from reproducing. Researchers believe that if helper T cells—HIV's main target—carry this artificial enzyme, they cannot be infected.

The question was, how could researchers get the blood cells to start making this special ribozyme? The answer, they hoped, could be found in the stem cells in the participants' bone marrow. These cells can form various kinds of blood cells to replace ones that have died or become worn out. The researchers removed stem cells from the patients' bone marrow and used a harmless virus to carry a new, ribozyme-producing gene into the cells. About 90 percent of the treated stem cells carried the new gene, and so did all the blood cells that they formed. When the modified stem cells were injected back into the participants in the study, they produced T cells that could fight disease germs without becoming infected by HIV.

What Are Stem Cells?

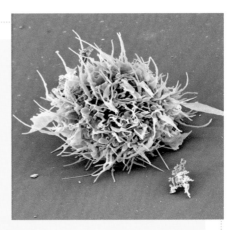

All the cells in your body started off as stem cells. Stem cells are immature cells that have the potential to grow into any kind of cells or tissues in the body. The cells in very early embryos (just a few days after the egg is fertilized) are all stem cells. Even in adults, a tiny fraction of the cells in the bone marrow, liver, spleen, and other tissues are stem cells. Such stem cells may be called upon to form red blood cells, which look like little doughnut-shaped disks, or white blood cells that are like tiny animated blobs of jelly. In the laboratory, using different kinds of nutrients and growth factors, scientists have made bone marrow stem cells divide into cells typical of different kinds of tissues—muscle or nerve cells, for example. Stem cells can also be modified (changed slightly) by genetic engineering to produce new chemicals. When the modified stem cells are inserted into a patient's body, these chemicals can help to correct a hereditary disorder or treat a disease.

Less than ten months after receiving the treatment, Michael was able to stop taking all his antiviral drugs. He did not know whether he was among the group that had received the anti-HIV gene or the group that had been given their own, unchanged stem cells back again. However, what he did know was that his T-cell count had doubled, and his HIV viral load had become "undetectable." Michael was feeling healthy and strong again.

At the time of Michael's first anniversary without anti-HIV drugs, other participants in the study were also showing positive results. However, they had not yet gone long enough to be sure that the treatment was working.[1]

Although this study seems very promising, it is a very high-tech method, and the treatment is custom-made for each individual patient. Eventually researchers may be able to mass-produce modified stem cells that can be given to anyone, which would make this kind of treatment much cheaper and more widely available. For the near future, however, most AIDS treatments will be based on the use of antiviral drugs.

Research on AIDS drugs today is focused on finding more effective drugs that attack HIV in different ways.

Research on AIDS drugs today is focused on finding more effective drugs that attack HIV in different ways. This approach may also help to solve one of the main problems in AIDS treatment today—drug resistance.

Overcoming Drug Resistance

AZT was the first anti-HIV drug to be discovered and used for treating AIDS patients. It worked fairly well at first, and many of the patients began to get better. Soon, however, doctors found that often the drug stopped working. The virus multiplied, and patients who had been taking AZT got sick again. The reason was that AZT did not kill all the virus particles. Some of them changed to become resistant to AZT.

AIDS researchers were still hard at work, though. They soon produced a number of chemicals that were a little different from AZT but worked in much the same way. Like AZT, they prevented cells infected with HIV from building complete DNA copies of the virus genes. However, the virus kept mutating (changing its genes), and soon strains resistant to the new drugs appeared. The same thing happened when different kinds of AIDS drugs were developed. Treatments were more successful when doctors learned to give HIV-infected patients

The HIV Life Cycle

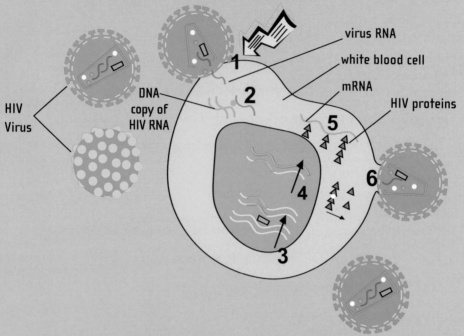

Step 1: Binding. HIV attaches to CD4 and other proteins on the surface of a white blood cell, and then its RNA enters the cell. Drugs called entry inhibitors can block this step.

Step 2: Reverse Transcription. The infected cell makes a DNA copy of the HIV RNA. This step can be blocked by nucleoside antivirals (artificial compounds similar to the building blocks of DNA) and by non-nucleoside reverse transcriptase inhibitors (NNRTIs).

several different kinds of drugs all at once. The "drug cocktails" usually include drugs that attack HIV in at least three different ways. It is very hard for the virus to make enough changes, fast enough, to survive.

Drug-resistant strains are still a problem, however. Researchers are trying to solve the problem by developing

Step 3: Integration. HIV "tricks" an infected cell into making new virus particles by hiding the DNA copies of its genes among the cell's own genes. When the cell makes new proteins, it accidentally makes virus proteins. Drugs called integrase inhibitors stop this step and were being tested in 2007.

Step 4: Transcription. When a cell makes proteins, it first makes RNA copies of the genes that contain the protein-making instructions. This type of copying is called transcription. The RNA produced is called messenger RNA (mRNA). (It carries the protein-making "message.") In 2007, drugs to stop this step were in early stages of development. These drugs are called transcription inhibitors.

Step 5: Translation. The infected cell uses the mRNA to make HIV proteins.

Step 6: Viral Assembly and Maturation. Long strings of protein are cut up by an enzyme called protease into shorter proteins. Some of them are enzymes; others are building blocks. They are put together with HIV RNA to form new virus particles. Drugs called protease inhibitors block this assembly process.

When new HIV particles first leave an infected cell, they are not yet able to infect other cells. The virus proteins have to go through some changes, called maturation, to become infectious. Drugs called maturation inhibitors were being developed in 2007 to stop this final process of the HIV life cycle.

drugs to target different steps in the virus's life cycle. In the first step, for example, an HIV particle attaches to the outer membrane of a cell, and its genetic information enters the cell. A drug named Fuzeon was approved by the FDA in 2003. It was the first of a new type of AIDS drugs called entry inhibitors. It blocks a protein on the cell membrane that HIV normally uses to latch on, and thus stops the virus from attaching to blood cells.[2] Drug companies are working on other new entry inhibitors, such as ribozymes. The ribozymes being developed as anti-HIV drugs stop cells from making the surface proteins that HIV uses to attach to and enter them.[3]

Other drugs now being studied work on different steps of the HIV life cycle, as shown in the illustration on pages 92–93.[4]

Efforts to Save Lives

Improved AIDS treatments have dramatically cut the numbers of people dying of AIDS in the United States and other industrialized countries. Most of the people infected with HIV, however, live in nonindustrialized countries in sub-Saharan Africa and Asia. Most of them cannot get the latest AIDS drugs—or even any treatments at all. According to World Health Organization (WHO) officials, as of December 2005, only 20 percent of people needing treatment in low- and middle-income countries were actually receiving it. Fewer than 10 percent of HIV-infected pregnant women were getting treatments to prevent passing the virus to their babies.[5]

Public health agencies, private foundations, and drug companies are working together to help make treatments more widely available. Companies producing antiviral drugs sell them at special reduced prices to nonindustrialized countries. Local programs are helping to make medical services more available to people in cities and remote villages. The UN-sponsored "3 by 5" campaign (three million under treatment by the end of 2005) did not reach its goal, but it tripled the number of people with access to AIDS drugs, from 400,000 to 1.3 million. If the number of AIDS cases continues to grow, however, there is no way these services can keep up with the epidemic. Better ways of *preventing* new HIV infections are needed. As Dr. Seth Berkley, director of the International AIDS Vaccine Initiative, puts it, "If we don't get serious about prevention, the demand for drugs will drown us."[6]

Education about AIDS and how the spread of HIV can be prevented is an important part of the fight against AIDS, especially in nonindustrialized countries. In Thailand, which reported its first AIDS case

Education about AIDS and how the spread of HIV can be prevented is an important part of the fight against AIDS, especially in nonindustrialized countries.

in 1984, a "100 percent condom program" was launched in 1991. The program urged the use of condoms for *every* sexual contact. The HIV infection rate had already begun to fall by 1994, especially in high-risk groups.[7]

Reaching Out to the World's Teens

AIDS is a worldwide epidemic, and health experts all over the world are targeting teenagers with kid-friendly education efforts. In South Africa, for example, teens used to get very little information about sex. When President Nelson Mandela mentioned safe sex in a speech, parents complained that he would give their children "bad ideas," so he stopped talking about it for years. The spread of AIDS began to change these views, but a poll reported in 2002 found that only 22 percent of teenagers had learned about sex from their parents. (Seventy percent said they wished they had.) Educators are trying to spread the word about safe sex through a popular TV and radio soap opera, *Soul City*, set in a township clinic. Each year, when a new series of episodes begins, a million comic books based on the series are inserted in daily newspapers around the nation. The show also produces a ninth-grade life skills textbook and Soul Buddyz books and tapes for eight- to twelve-year-olds that reach about two-thirds of those students. In rural areas, where it is difficult to get books and tapes, schools put on annual plays about AIDS.[8]

In Africa, Uganda led the way, setting up AIDS prevention programs in the early 1990s. AIDS education focused on abstaining, being faithful to one partner, and using condoms. Rates of HIV infection had dropped sharply by the late 1990s and were continuing to fall in the 2000s. A scientific study reported in 2004 found that HIV infection rates in Uganda had fallen 70 percent. There had also been major changes in people's behavior: "Casual sex" had decreased by 60 percent.[9] HIV infection rates had also begun to fall in other parts of east and central Africa. In Kenya, for example, there has been a 50 percent drop since the mid-1990s, according to Peter Piot, the director of UNAIDS.[10]

The Quest for an AIDS Vaccine

Why isn't there a vaccine against AIDS yet? After all, we have vaccines that protect people from getting many viral and bacterial diseases, such as polio and measles. The vaccine against smallpox was so effective that no one receives the vaccine anymore! There has not been a case of smallpox since 1977.

The vaccines that protect us from various diseases are aimed at getting the body to produce antibodies. That approach was not very effective against HIV,

Dr. Juliana McElrath of the Fred Hutchinson Cancer Research Center is lead researcher and part of a collaborative effort of international scientists who are studying the development of an HIV vaccine.

however. HIV attacks the immune system itself, especially the helper T cells. These white blood cells normally help B cells produce antibodies, and they also help in the work of the killer T cells. As HIV infects and kills helper T cells, the other parts of the immune system become less able to work effectively. Moreover, HIV mutates often, producing slightly different surface chemicals that the immune cells may not be able to recognize. In addition, some of its key surface chemicals are covered with a coating of sugar that hides them from attacking antibodies. People who are infected with HIV do make antibodies against the virus, but these antibodies usually do not work well enough to keep the infection under control.

Eventually, researchers realized they needed to focus on a vaccine that makes the body produce new killer T cells to stop the infection from spreading. In 2007, a new vaccine was being tested in eighteen cities around the world. The vaccine combines three important HIV genes with a common cold virus. The cold virus is disabled so that it can infect people but cannot make them sick. The vaccine cannot give people AIDS because they receive only a small part of the HIV genes, not the whole AIDS virus.[11] Most other vaccines are based on a killed or weakened form of the germ causing the disease. This is too risky to do with AIDS. A killed vaccine might accidentally contain a few particles of live virus, or a weakened form might mutate into a stronger, deadly virus.

Researchers expect that the first AIDS vaccines might not be completely successful in protecting people from HIV infection. However, they believe these vaccines may work well enough to keep the viral load small.

Then the infected person's immune system will be able to keep the infection under control, and he or she will not develop symptoms of full-blown AIDS.[12]

* * *

There have been many amazing advances in AIDS research since the disease first appeared. New types of drugs are already helping many people with HIV/AIDS to live longer than ever before, greatly increasing their chances of survival. Efforts to increase education on AIDS prevention have also had a big impact on lowering the number of people getting infected in the first place. Being smart about AIDS can help keep people safe.

Questions and Answers

A boy in my class is HIV positive. Can I get the virus when he coughs? No. The AIDS virus is not like a cold virus. It is not spread through the air or even by touching a doorknob or a towel an infected person has touched.

I heard you can get AIDS by "sexual contact." Does that include kissing? Possibly, but it's not very likely. A friendly kiss is safe, but a long, deep, openmouthed kiss could possibly transmit the AIDS virus if both people have mouth sores or bleeding gums. No cases known to be transmitted this way have been reported, however.

Can you get AIDS if you have sex just once? Yes. Your chances of becoming infected with HIV increase with the number of sex partners, as well as with the number of times a person has sex. However, people have become infected after just one sexual experience with an infected partner.

Is sex safe as long as people use a condom? Using condoms makes sex safer, but there is a chance that condoms may leak or break. The only completely "safe sex" is abstinence—no sexual contact with a partner at all.

I just found out that my big sister had sex with someone who is HIV positive. Should she get tested for AIDS? Yes. And if the test is negative, she should be tested again six months later to make sure.

Can people infected with HIV ever have kids? Yes. These days, there are medicines pregnant women can take that lower the risk of passing the virus to their baby. HIV-positive men can use a method called "sperm washing" to remove virus-infected sperm cells. The HIV-free sperm cells that remain will not carry a risk of infection to either the mother or child.

My mom tried to give blood, but they said her blood tested HIV positive. Does she have AIDS? Not necessarily. People who are infected with HIV may live for many years before they develop symptoms of AIDS. And the test may not be accurate. She should have another test done to make sure.

HIV/AIDS Timeline

1930s A virus found in primates, SIV, is believed to have jumped to humans in Africa when they killed infected chimpanzees and monkeys for meat. The virus later became HIV.

1959 First known case of HIV (confirmed by tests in 1998) is found in a man from Congo.

1969 Teenager Robert R. dies of AIDS (confirmed by tests in 1986) in St. Louis.

1981 Unusual immune system problems are first reported in American gay men; Gay Men's Health Crisis (first AIDS organization) is founded.

1982 The new disease is named Acquired Immune Deficiency Syndrome (AIDS).

1983 AIDS is reported in two women who caught it from sex partners; pediatrician James Oleske reports on cases of AIDS in children; U.S. researcher Robert Gallo and French researcher Luc Montagnier both report finding viruses linked to AIDS.

1984 .... Robert Gallo grows the AIDS virus in culture and develops techniques for detecting antibodies to it; French team also develops a blood test.

1985 .... First AIDS antibody test is approved in the United States; HIV screening of blood donations begins; actor Rock Hudson becomes the first big celebrity to disclose he has AIDS.

1986 .... AIDS virus is named HIV (*H*uman *I*mmunodeficiency *V*irus).

1987 .... FDA approves AZT (first anti-AIDS drug) for use in the United States.

1988 .... First World AIDS Day; the first New York needle-exchange program is started.

1991 .... The red ribbon becomes an international symbol of AIDS awareness; pro basketball player Magic Johnson announces that he is HIV positive.

1993 .... The vaginal pouch (female condom) is approved by the FDA.

1994 .... NIH announces that AZT treatment lowers the risk of HIV transfer from mother to infant.

1995 .... Two kinds of AIDS drugs, protease inhibitors and non-nucleoside reverse transcriptase inhibitors, are shown to greatly reduce viral load.

1996 .... FDA approves first HIV home test kit.

1997 .... FDA approves the first drug combination pill, Combivir (AZT + 3TC).

1998 .... The U.S. Supreme Court states that in addition to people with AIDS, those infected with HIV are covered under the Americans with Disabilities Act, even if they do not show symptoms.

1999 .... The American Medical Association (AMA) adopts a policy stating public schools should teach condom use as well as abstinence in sex education classes as a way to prevent the spread of AIDS and other STDs.

2002 .... The FDA approves a rapid finger-prick HIV antibody test.

2003 .... Fuzeon, the first entry inhibitor, is approved by the FDA.

2006 .... June 5 is the 25th anniversary of the first reported AIDS cases; the FDA approves the first once-a-day AIDS drug, called Atripla (combines three drugs in one).

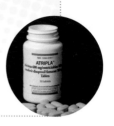

For More Information

ACT UP (AIDS Coalition to Unleash Power)
332 Bleecker St., Suite G5
New York, NY 10014
Email: actupny@panix.com
Web site: http://www.actupny.org/

AIDSinfo
P.O. Box 6303
Rockville, MD 20849-6303
Email: ContactUs@aidsinfo.nih.gov
Live help: http://aidsinfo.nih.gov/LiveHelp/
Web site: http://aidsinfo.nih.gov/
Toll-free: 1-800-HIV-0440 (1-800-448-0440)

Centers for Disease Control and Prevention
1600 Clifton Road, NE
Atlanta, GA 30333
404-639-3534
Web site: http://www.cdc.gov/
Toll free: 1-800-311-3435

Gay Men's Health Crisis
The Tisch Building
119 West 24 Street
New York, NY 10011
Web site: http://www.gmhc.org/
Hotline: 212-807-6655
Toll-free: 1-800-AIDS-NYC (1-800-243-7692)

National Association of People With AIDS
8401 Colesville Road
Suite 750
Silver Spring, MD 20910
Email: info@napwa.org
Web site: http://www.napwa.org/
Phone: 240-247-0880
Fax: 240-247-0574

National Institute of Allergy and Infectious Diseases
NIAID Office of Communications and Public Liaison
6610 Rockledge Drive, MSC 6612
Bethesda, MD 20892-6612
Web site: http://www3.niaid.nih.gov/research/topics/
HIV/default.htm
Phone: 301-496-5717

World Health Organization (WHO)
World Health Organization Department
of HIV/AIDS
Avenue Appia, 20
CH-1211 Geneva 27
Switzerland
Email: hiv-aids@who.int
Web site: http://www.who.int/hiv/en/

Chapter Notes

Chapter 1. The Changing Face of AIDS

1. Carl Swanson, "The Coming Out of Regan Hofmann," *New York* magazine, June 5, 2006, <http://www.newyorkmetro.com/news/features/17142/> (June 28, 2006).

2. Ibid.

3. "Worldwide HIV & AIDS Statistics," *Avert*, December 6, 2006, <http://www.avert.org/worldstats.htm> (December 11, 2006).

4. National Institutes of Health, "HIV Infection and AIDS: An Overview," March 2005, <http://www.niaid.nih.gov/factsheets/hivinf.htm> (July 6, 2006).

Chapter 2. The History of AIDS

1. Randy Shilts, *And the Band Played On* (New York: Quality Paperback Book Club, 1993), pp. 42–43, 48–49, 55–56, 61–63.

2. Ibid., pp. 66–68.

3. Ibid., pp. 83, 147.

Chapter 3. What Is AIDS?

1. Johnny Guaylupo, "Personal Statement on Abstinence Programming," *Housing Works Advocacy*, November 1, 2005, <http://www.hwadvocacy.com/update/downloads/baltimore_jg_speech.pdf> (July 19, 2006).

2. Ibid.

3. Tim Murphy, Philip F. Rose, Michael Kink, and others, "Young, Gifted and Positive," *Housing Works Advocacy*, February 21, 2006, <http://www.hwadvocacy.com/update/archives/2006/02/young_gifted_an.html> (July 19, 2006).

Chapter 4. Diagnosis and Treatment

1. CNN.com, "Then & Now: Magic Johnson," June 22, 2005, <http://www.cnn.com/2005/US/01/17/cnn25.tan.johnson/index.html> (July 10, 2006).

2. Ibid.

3. "The New Faces of HIV/AIDS," *The Oprah Winfrey Show*, October 26, 2006 [transcript], <http://www.oprah.com/tows/slide/200610/20061026/slide_20061026_350_101.jhtml> (November 13, 2006).

4. Jonel Aleccia, "Quick HIV Test Available: Results Take Only 20 Minutes," *The Spokesman-Review*, June 27, 2006, <http://www.healthdecisions.org/HealthIT/News/default.aspx?doc_id=72183> (July 27, 2006).

5. Centers for Disease Control and Prevention, "OraQuick Rapid HIV Test for Oral Fluid," April 26, 2004, <http://www.thebody.com/cdc/oraquick_faq.html> (July 27, 2006).

6. Rita Jenkins, "FDA Approves One-a-Day HIV-AIDS Pill," *Daily News Central: Health News*, July 14, 2006, <http://health.dailynewscentral.com/content/view/0002348/31/> (July 28, 2006).

7. Shamus Toomey and Rummana Hussain, "Oprah, Bono Spree to Support 'Red' HIV Cause," *Chicago Sun-Times,* October 13, 2006, <http://www.suntimes.com/news/metro/95226,CST-NWS-oprah13.article> (December 1, 2006).

Chapter 5. Living With HIV/AIDS

1. Delma J. Francis, "Hydeia Broadbent, 17, Has AIDS, but It Doesn't Define Her," *Star Tribune,* December 27, 2001, <http://www.aegis.com/news/ads/2001/AD012241.html> (July 19, 2006).

2. Twila Decker, "Not Too Young to Battle AIDS: Speech: Hydeia Broadbent, only 16, wages her own fight against the disease that has infected her. She tells people at a church event that it could happen to them," *Los Angeles Times,* March 11, 2001, <http://www.aegis.com/news/It/2001/LT010301.html> (July 19, 2006).

3. Kate Snow, "Progress for Some, Hopelessness for Many," *ABC News,* June 5, 2006, <http://abcnews.go.com/GMA/Health/story?id=203804&page=1> (July 31, 2006).

4. Katharine Q. Seelye, "Helms Puts the Brakes to a Bill Financing AIDS Treatment," *The New York Times,* July 5, 1995, <http://query.nytimes.com/gst/fullpage.html?sec=health&res=990CE4DA1230F936A35754C0A963958260> (August 1, 2006)

5. Mark Cichocki, "Is HIV/AIDS a Disability?" *About: HIV/AIDS,* July 13, 2006, <http://aids.about.com/od/legalissues/a/disability.htm> (August 16, 2006).

6. Associated Press, "Helms Sorry on AIDS, Not Race," *CBSNews.com*, June 9, 2005, <http://www.cbsnews.com/stories/2005/06/09/politics/main700682.shtml> (August 1, 2006).

7. "Policy Facts: AIDS-Related Stigma," *The Body: The Complete HIV/AIDS Resource*, January 2001, <http://www.thebody.com/aac/brochures/stigma.html> (July 27, 2006).

Chapter 6. Preventing AIDS

1. Andrea King Collier, "Over the Down Low," *Real Health Magazine*, Winter 2005/2006, <http://www.realhealthmag.com/articles/421_2441.shtml> (July 5, 2006).

2. Ibid.

3. Ben Cogswell, "To Be Young, Smart and HIV-Infected: Living a Positive Life," *Sex, etc. Magazine*, June 21, 2006, <http://www.sexetc.org/story/2231> (July 5, 2006).

4. Centers for Disease Control, "Basic Statistics," *CDC HIV/AIDS*, January 10, 2007, <http://www.cdc.gov/hiv/topics/surveillance/basic.htm> (February 5, 2007).

5. Gerald Stine, *AIDS UPDATE: 2005* (San Francisco, CA: Pearson Education, Inc., 2005), p. 255.

6. Drug Policy Alliance, "Sterile Syringe Access (Needle Exchange)," *Reducing Harm: Treatment and Beyond*, May 22, 2006, <http://www.lindesmith.org/reducingharm/needleexchan/> (August 8, 2006).

7. Steve LeBlanc, "Bill Would Allow Sale of Syringes Without a Prescription," *Associated Press,* November 14, 2005, <http://www.aegis.com/news/ap/2005/AP051132.html> (August 8, 2006).

8. Drug Policy Alliance.

9. National Institutes of Health, "Studies Shed New Light on Mother-to-Infant HIV Transmission," June 19, 1996, <http://www3.niaid.nih.gov/news/newsreleases/1996/wits.htm> (August 9, 2006).

10. Gina Kolata, "Discovery That AIDS Can Be Prevented in Babies Raises Debate on Mandatory Testing," *The New York Times,* November 5, 1994, <http://query.nytimes.com/gst/fullpage.html?sec=health&res=9E02E5DD173EF930A35752C1A962958260> (August 9, 2006).

11. March of Dimes, "HIV and AIDS in Pregnancy," November 2002, <http://www.marchofdimes.com/professionals/681_1223.asp> (August 8, 2006).

12. CDC, "Recommendations for Preventing Transmission of Human Immunodeficiency Virus and Hepatitis B Virus to Patients During Exposure-Prone Invasive Procedures," *MMWR,* July 12, 1991, pp. 1–9, <http://www.cdc.gov/mmwR/preview/mmwrhtml/00014845.htm> (February 5, 2007).

13. CDC, "Overview: Risks and Prevention of Sharps Injuries in Healthcare Personnel," *Workbook for Designing, Implementing, and Evaluating a Sharps Injury Prevention Program,* February 12, 2004, <http://www.cdc.gov/sharpssafety/wk_overview.html> (February 5, 2007).

14. Carol Ann Campbell, "The Youngest Patients Keep a Pioneering Doctor Busy," *The Star-Ledger* (Newark, NJ), July 18, 2006, pp. 1, 6.

Chapter 7. AIDS and the Future

1. Sabin Russell, "High Hopes For AIDS Therapy: Experimental Treatment Fortifies the Body's Own Stem Cells with an Enzyme that could Block the Virus' Relentless Advance," *San Francisco Chronicle*, April 7, 2006, <http://www.sfgate.com/cgi-bin/article.cgi?f=/c/a/2006/04/07/MNGH6I59Q61.DTL&hw=Sabin+Russell+High+Hopes+for+AIDS+Therapy&sn=003&sc=538> (December 11, 2006).

2. Patrick McGee, "A Quarter Century of Battling HIV/AIDS," *Drug Discovery and Development*, July 2006, pp. 10–18; Graham Allaway, "HIV/AIDS Drug Resistance," Ibid., p. 52.

3. MMI Group, "Ribozyme Anti-Virals," ©2006, <http://mmigroup.co.uk/mmi/viratis.jsp?n=6&s=24> (August 5, 2006).

4. Howard Grossman, Medical Editor of AIDSmeds.com, "The HIV Life Cycle," December 1, 2005, <http://www.aidsmeds.com/lessons/LifeCycleIntro.htm> and following links (August 4, 2006).

5. "The Global HIV/AIDS Pandemic, 2006," *MMWR (Morbidity and Mortality Weekly Report)*, August 11, 2006, pp. 841–844, <http://www.cdc.gov/mmwr/preiew/mmwrhtml/mm5531a1.htm> (August 11, 2006).

6. Geoffrey Cowley, "The Life of a Virus Hunter," *Newsweek*, May 15, 2006, p. 64.

7. Jon Cohen, "Two Hard-Hit Countries Offer Rare Success Stories," *Science,* September 19, 2003, pp. 1658–1662.

8. Donald G. McNeil, Jr., "On Stages and Screens, AIDS Educators Reach South Africa's Youths," Health Systems Trust, from a *New York Times* article, February 3, 2002, Section 1, page 6, <http://new.hst.org.za/news/index.php/20020212/> (August 18, 2006).

9. Rand L. Stoneburner and Daniel Low-Beer, "Population-Level HIV Declines and Behavioral Risk Avoidance in Uganda," *Science,* April 30, 2004, pp. 714–718.

10. Cowley.

11. "Merck's Investigational HIV/AIDS Vaccine Advances to Phase II Efficacy Testing in Collaborative Clinical Trial," January 24, 2005, <http://www.hvtn.org/media/press_releases.sht?id=41> (August 18, 2006).

12. Tom Paulson, "Seattle Scientists Expand Testing of AIDS Vaccine," *Seattle Post-Intelligencer,* January 25, 2005, <http://seattlepi.nwsource.com/local/209222_aidsvax25.html> (August 18, 2006).

Glossary

abstinence—Not having any sexual contact with a partner.

anal sex—Sexual activity in which the penis of one partner is inserted into the rectum of another.

antibody—A protein that is produced to attach specifically to surface chemicals on a virus that has invaded the body.

antibody test—A diagnostic test to detect the presence of antibodies to a particular germ in blood or saliva, which confirms the presence or absence of the germ.

antiviral drugs—Medicines that work to kill or disable viruses.

AZT—The first anti-HIV drug approved; a nucleoside reverse transcriptase inhibitor; also called zidovudine (brand name Retrovir).

B cells—White blood cells that produce antibodies against germs and foreign substances.

CD4—A protein on the surface of helper T cells, to which HIV binds when it invades a cell.

combination cocktail—A combination of drugs used to treat HIV/AIDS.

condom—A thin covering placed over the penis during sexual intercourse to prevent pregnancy and the spread of disease. (Only rubber condoms prevent the spread of HIV infection.)

DNA (deoxyribonucleic acid)—A substance that carries the hereditary instructions for making proteins.

drug resistance—The ability of a disease germ to survive and multiply in the presence of a drug that would ordinarily kill or disable it.

entry inhibitors—Drugs that block a protein on the cell membrane that HIV normally uses to latch on, and thus stop the virus from attaching to blood cells.

gay—A popular term for homosexual (usually male).

gene—A chemical unit containing coded instructions for the formation of a protein; genes determine hereditary traits passed on from one generation to the next.

HAART (highly active antiretroviral therapy)—Treatment that involves a combination of drugs (called a "cocktail"), usually including two reverse transcriptase inhibitors and one or two protease inhibitors.

helper T cells—White blood cells that help some cells of the immune system to make antibodies and others to attack virus-infected cells; also called CD4 cells.

hemophilia—A hereditary blood disorder in which blood does not clot normally.

heterosexual—A person who is attracted to persons of the opposite sex.

HIV (human immunodeficiency virus)—A virus that attacks the immune system and may eventually lead to AIDS.

homosexual—A person who is attracted to persons of the same sex.

host—A living plant or animal that provides food and shelter for another creature.

immune system—The body's defense-fighting system, which includes the white blood cells.

injection drug user—A person who uses drugs, such as heroin, taken by injection into a vein.

integrase inhibitors—Drugs that block the integration process.

integration—The process by which HIV "tricks" an infected cell into making new virus particles by hiding the DNA copies of its genes among the cell's own genes.

Kaposi's sarcoma—A skin cancer that produces purplish spots.

killer T cells—White blood cells that recognize and attack virus-infected cells; also called CD8 cells.

lymph nodes—Bean-sized organs consisting mostly of densely packed white blood cells, clustered in the armpits, groin, and various other parts of the body.

maturation—The final processing of new HIV viruses to make them capable of infecting cells.

maturation inhibitors—Drugs that prevent maturation of new HIV viruses.

messenger RNA—An RNA copy of a DNA gene that carries its information to the protein-making sites in cells.

monogamous—Having only one sex partner at a time.

non-nucleoside reverse transcriptase inhibitors (NNRTIs)—Drugs that block the cell from making a DNA copy of HIV's RNA but are not similar to the normal DNA building blocks (nucleosides).

nucleoside antivirals—Drugs similar to the normal DNA building blocks (nucleosides) that prevent infected cells from making a DNA copy of HIV's RNA.

opportunistic infection—An illness caused by a virus, bacterium, or parasite that produces symptoms only in people whose immune defenses are already weakened.

oral sex—Sexual activity involving contact between the mouth of one partner and the sex organs of the other.

PCP (Pneumocystis carinii pneumonia)—An opportunistic lung infection caused by a protozoa-like fungus.

protease—An enzyme that cuts large proteins into smaller proteins.

protease inhibitor—A drug that blocks the action of HIV protease, an enzyme that cuts long protein strands into functional HIV proteins.

retrovirus—A virus that contains genetic information in the form of RNA, which is used as a pattern for the host cell to manufacture DNA (genes), which then directs the production of virus materials.

reverse transcriptase inhibitor—A drug that blocks the action of the HIV enzyme reverse transcriptase, which directs the formation of DNA copies of viral RNA.

ribozyme—An enzyme that is made of RNA instead of protein.

RNA (ribonucleic acid)—A substance that is similar to DNA but has a simpler structure. Several types of RNA are involved in making proteins.

semen—Fluid containing sperm, released from the penis during sexual activity.

sex organ—A body part used for reproduction; also called genital organs or genitals.

sexual intercourse—Sexual activity involving contact of the sex organs; sometimes called vaginal sex.

sexually transmitted disease (STD)—Any disease that can be transferred from one partner to another usually as a result of vaginal, oral, or anal sex.

SIV (simian immunodeficiency virus)—A retrovirus found in monkeys (simians) that is closely related to HIV.

stem cells—Immature cells that have the potential for developing into any type of cell or tissue.

stigma—Shame or disgrace attached to something regarded as socially unacceptable.

transcription—The process of making an RNA copy of part of a cell's DNA.

transcription inhibitors—Drugs that prevent the transcription process from being completed.

vaginal sex—Sexual activity in which the penis of the male partner is inserted into the vagina of the female partner.

viral load—The amount of virus present in the blood.

wasting syndrome—Severe unintentional weight loss (mainly loss of muscle tissue).

Further Reading

Broadbent, Patricia, Patricia Romanowski, and Hydeia Broadbent. *You Get Past the Tears: A Memoir of Love and Survival.* New York: Villard Books, 2002.

Brynie, Faith Hickman. *101 Questions About Your Immune System You Felt Defenseless to Answer—Until Now.* Brookfield, Conn.: Twenty-First Century Books, 2000.

Ellis, Deborah. *Our Stories, Our Songs: African Children Talk About AIDS.* Markham, Ont.: Fitzhenry & Whiteside, 2005.

Farrell, Jeanette. *Invisible Enemies: Stories of Infectious Diseases.* New York: Farrar, Straus, Giroux, 2005.

Hinds, Maurene J. *Fighting the AIDS and HIV Epidemic: A Global Battle.* Berkeley Heights, NJ: Enslow Publishers, Inc., 2007.

Howard, Helen. *Living with AIDS: Mary's Story.* Milwaukee: World Almanac Library, 2006.

Routh, Kristina. *AIDS.* Milwaukee: World Almanac Library, 2005.

Watstein, Sarah Barbara, and Stephen E. Stratton. *The Encyclopedia of HIV and AIDS.* New York: Facts on File, 2003.

White, Katherine. *Everything You Need to Know About AIDS and HIV.* New York: The Rosen Publishing Group, Inc., 2001.

Internet Addresses

(See also **For More Information**, p. 107.)

American Social Health Association. "Answers to Your Questions About Teen Sexual Health and Sexually Transmitted Diseases."
http://www.iwannaknow.org

National Center for HIV, STD and TB Prevention. "HIV and AIDS: Are You at Risk?"
**http://www.cdc.gov/hiv/resources/brochures/
     at-risk.htm**

Unicef Voices of Youth. "Be in the Know: How Can You Help Stop the Spread of HIV?"
http://www.unicef.org/voy/explore/aids/explore_aids.php

Index

M

MAC (*Mycobacterium avium* complex), 43

Mandela, Nelson, 96

maturation, 93

maturation inhibitors, 93

McElrath, Juliana, **98**

mental health, 69

Mercury, Freddie, 32

messenger RNA (mRNA), 93

monkeys, 26, 103

monogamous relationship, 37

Montagnier, Luc, 25, 103

Morbidity and Mortality Weekly Report (MMWR), 19

mother-to-child transmission of HIV, 35, 81, 82, 94, 104

mutation, 26, 91, 98

N

Nashville CARES, 74

National Association of People With AIDS, 108

National Cancer Institute (NCI), 24

National Institute of Allergy and Infectious Diseases (NIAID), 108

needle-exchange programs (NEPs), 79–87, 104

needlestick injuries, 83

New York City schools, 78

night sweats, 42

nonindustrialized countries, 94, 95

non-nucleoside reverse transcriptase inhibitors (NNRTIs), 52, 92, 105

nucleoside antivirals, 52, 92

O

Oleske, James, 84–85, **84**, 103

opportunistic infections, 20, 21, 33, 34, 42, 43, 50, 52, 53, 55

prevention of, 53

oral HIV test, 48

oral sex, 34

OraQuick HIV test, 48

P

Pacific region, 13

"Patient Zero," 21

PCP (Pneumocystis carinii pneumonia), 18, 20, 34, 43, 53

pediatric AIDS, 84–85

Piot, Peter, 97

pneumonia, 7, 42, 61, 73

POZ magazine, 8, 9, 11, 12

pregnant women, 81–82

protease, 93

protease inhibitors, 52–53, 93, 105

protein, 70

R

Rambo, Dack, 32

rectum, 34

red blood cells, 89

Red Campaign, 56, 57

Red Cross Spirit Award, 61

red ribbon, 104

Reed, Robert, 32

retrovirus, 121

reverse transcriptase, 52

reverse transcription, 92

ribosomes, **40**

ribozyme, 88–90, 94

risk of HIV infection, 37

risk groups, 6, 75

RNA, **40, 92**
Robert R., 103
Ryan White CARE Act, 22

S

safe sex, 96
safer sex, 75–77, 78, 101
semen, 34, 37
Serrano, Yolanda, 79
sex education, 78, 96, 105
sexual contact, 101
sexual history, 73
Shilts, Randy, **21**
"shooting galleries," 77
SIV (simian immunodeficiency
     virus), 26, 103
sleep, 69–70
smallpox, 97
Soul Buddyz, 96
Soul City, 96
South Africa, **15**, 96
sperm washing, 102
STDs (sexually transmitted diseases),
     18, 20, 30, 35, 75
stem cells, 88–90, **89**
sub-Saharan Africa, 13, 94
support groups, 10, 71
support system, 70
syringes, 77, 80

T

Tasha Durant Award for Positive
     Leadership, 33
tattooing, 6
T-cell count, 90
Thailand, 95–96
Thorburn, Kim, 48
"3 by 5" campaign, 95

Toxoplasma, 42
toxoplasmosis, 43
transcription, 93
transcription inhibitors, 93
translation, 93
tuberculosis, 34, 80

U

Uganda, 97
United States Supreme Court, 65, 105
universal precautions, 83
University of California, San
     Francisco (UCSF), 88
unprotected sex, 27, 34, 72

V

vagina, 34
vaginal pouch, 76, 104
vaginal sex, 34, 37
viral assembly, 93
viral load, 31, 49, 50, 55, 87, 90,
     99, 105
virus reproduction, 39–41, **40**
viruses, 24, 33

W

Weisman, Joel, 18
white blood cell count, 31
white blood cells, 39, 40, 89, **92**
White, Ryan, **22**
Winfrey, Oprah, **56**, 57
World AIDS day, 104
World Health Organization (WHO),
     94, 108

Z

Zamora, Pedro, **32**